Nemo under the League

Vernon Frazer

Unlikely Books
www.UnlikelyStories.org
New Orleans, Louisiana

Unlikely Books
www.UnlikelyStories.org
New Orleans, Louisiana

Nemo under the League

cortical
plasma damage

repeating the swollen meat adagio
hoisted to their epicentral forefront
in plenary dispassion

SURMOUNTING

detunes
the serenade
on replay

the desperation of vesicle heat

appellative
quandary
buttons

a correlative
socket sprint

left tainted

tinting
the internal
blemish

as a
splinter
hilding
in the
testimonial

damage
the plasma vortex

distention
invasions
from their
renowned
master of
dissolution

entropic chant

ballad wizard

elliptical pin droppings

surreptitious voltage
clocked its tension rant
torn from the core

of a storm

raining against

CRIMINALLY BLUNTS

THE PLASMA CHEVRON

an image
courting plastic

attached its distillation
chart while slowly discharging

THE HUNT

from its bargain journey

trolling

THE VALLEY

through the lost epithets

with
their
drolls

THE CHASE

to guide the patrol

printing
a vesicle
pocket

maligned for

on the turret

off-topic rant

damaged

plasma

a vortex
recital

where the filigree
assets tongue the
tired remembrance

pocket lint

in reverse direction

asthmatic
soma probes
aromatic

no
direction
fits

an imaging
deterrent elastic

bit the socket

vestibular differential

the inferential image

split

at its core deferential

LACKED CEREMONIALS

release buttons
and
locktight armada

small change
in the superman booth

every nickle

dimed

HINT
POCKETS
LIFTED

a varied

escalation

no matter

the pick

through the hole

where eyeglasses
make a spectacle

nutriments breaking the number
landing their penumbral stickers
before the audio declension fits

brimming

neophyte drifter onstage

elation packet

delirium

derangement of the censors
where the postcards hanging
innocent victims on cling pits
estranged for their sentence

FOR
GALLOWS
HUMOR

AMNIOTIC INTRUSION REPORT

hordes insufficient data

rampage follows

the slow request

damage
ingress
as done

did not get won in the voltage
that elapsed

left
a trail
packaging

MEMORY TASKS

charity
lozenge
imprints

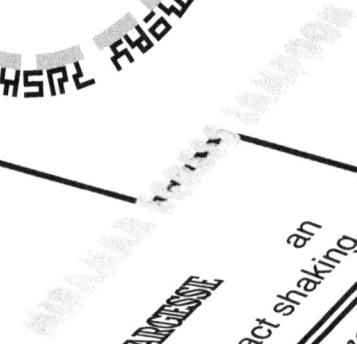

shake off the filter habit

CORPOREAL TERROVISUAL DISSOLVE

BUTTERFLY NARCISSE

an
impact shaking
in madras

augurs
a wives tale
ovary goat

SEMIOTIC TRANSITION SUPPORT

SPLENECTOMY BREATH

an
innocence
turned
molting

a cornered
incarnation
a madness

breaks the accord

a somnolent verity established

OVARY PUDDING

on a pancake ledge

with

legendary

husk

SEQUESTERED

a

cordial

egress

TACTILE

VERITIES

A REMOVAL TASK

A PORTABLE INDIGNATION RAMP

among brooding
hordes of homilies

lose

their

feathers

to modular dissemination

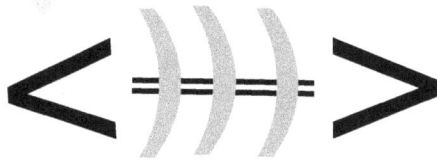

while mustard cavils

a word

castigates

ruddered
nonchalance

questing

VESTMENT

le
mot
du
jour

drives

to future *veritas* gardens

hidden

in vino

stemming
an entitled
fury patch

a vintage suite

lacking
tactical veracity

in the climate chutes

chilling
ultimatum fillers

where
leathers never hold
their counsel

A RAZOR UMBRA

RIPPLING
MUSCATEL

follows the voltage
of a semiotic tradition report

finding taste

a
fluid
issue

the conundrum village
imploding on a wet stack

of letter bafflements
that eclipsed

mustard filler

while bequeathing
the wives a goat
in accord to cavil

ECLIPSE
VERITAS

a
fictive
ingress

DIVESTMENT

tactile voracity candles

WRITHING
A
MERCY TIDE

the filler memorandum
a decibel file accord

the wet track scaffold
a movement eclipsed

the cavil mustered
rampage damage

over the sequester ledge
an amniotic transit button
pushed the circumference

until the lines

tasted

scaffold mustard

while
intrusions
hid

behind

the suffix mold

the coldness foretelling
cataleptic nuance crackers

chilling the climate chutes

WIDELY
INDIGNANT
DESPITE THE
PAMPERED
PANACEA
TALE

displaced and darkened
their avenued pursuit

unfolding
duplicate legends
astride
behemoth galleries

THE CHORUS
LEADS EVOLUTION
SCRAPS TO

DENIGRATION
COOPS
NOTWITHSTANDING

A
ACTIVE
EGRESS

reliving the vigor
of ice control under a surface bonnet

flatulent a capella no excuse

NO REQUIEM SURCHARGE REQUIRED

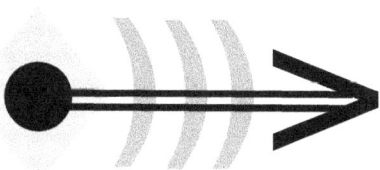

BRISTLES
INDIGNATION
CAMPERS

RASHING MEMORIES

frozen at the avenue crossing
where titillation reversals fall short of happening
garbanzo legends accrue

their feet a slow detachment ring
varnished
like a ravaged settlement

the reticular ruminant desires

BREATHING A CRAMPED RENDITION

stampede in hunger fury

CLAMPED TO THE ABSENCE OF

SURFACE

MEMORY MARSH

packaging
the trail left

the surcharge
a chilling requiem closure

insurgent thermostat accord
avuncular remix stations fester
glory gadgets in the offspring

clinging

to hirsute fabric

A RAMPED EDITION

decision

mustered their devils

decibel creation extravaganza

the page unleashed

TERMINAL

EXTRAVAGANCE

heroic flotation

patronymic effusion
captured in a surrogate
rafter

ELATION

symbiotic deviation device
a transfer to recreational impunity

slowing the mix

location revised

devised

obdurate
passions

platform
vindication

on transfer

**meat
thicket
reviled**

under
a grim translucence

a
tentacular
revision

reel aplomb

scrotal motoring

QUIESCENT STAMMER STRIKES

heel
stepping
out

a flotation device

riding
a sawtooth equation
its hunger
for

**OMNIVORE
HAMMER
FORCE**

liminal smithereens enlarged
the seminal force of a proxy gland

(heroic notation)

inscribed

a

nascent

predilection

clamored suture

an
oral
victim

the litany assuages
surrogate impunity
to minimal transfer

decimal variation
the pin flux effusion
of a surrogate

CANNED

captured

on a rafter

a
decimation
rotor

described

motorcade

thick
meat
rebelled

(heroic flotation)

turning
Its take
from a

prosaic rotation

scrotal rotary
rafter dissuasion

paroxysmal refusal
ushered in a surrogate
as its

an
oral
icon

FIXATION

slowed the mix

talking moral impunity
a recreational transfer
captured in a slowing
tentacular rafter litany

heel
stepping
on

libation

repelled

location proxy

Blocking the Inevitable

COLLEGIAL TRANSFERENCE

BARRICADING

sells wolf tickets
before the pack house
backs
opprobrium jackets
bracketing
new shades
of deferral

ADEQUATE WANDERING MESSAGES

DEOXACENVIED RETRIBUTION POCKET

a foregone template armada

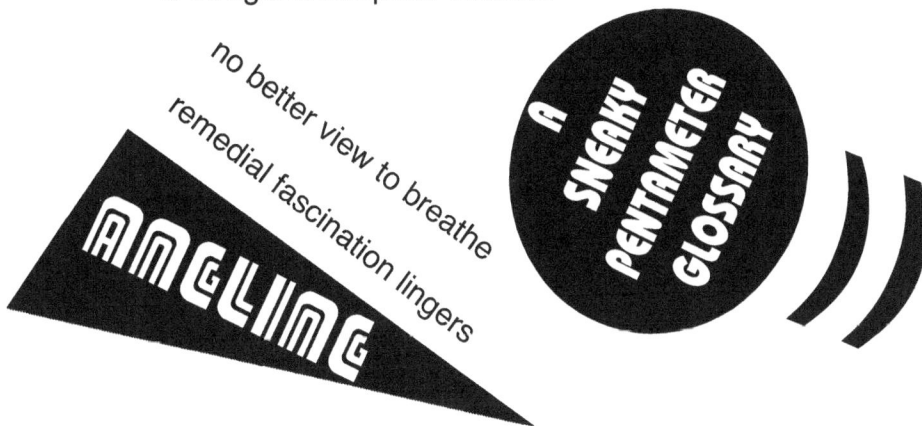

no better view to breathe
remedial fascination lingers

ANGLING

A SNEAKY PENTAMETER GLOSSARY

forced a meter to guide them
past the follicles of envy
no hirsute longing
transport
left to methodology

and other
barriers to entropic replay

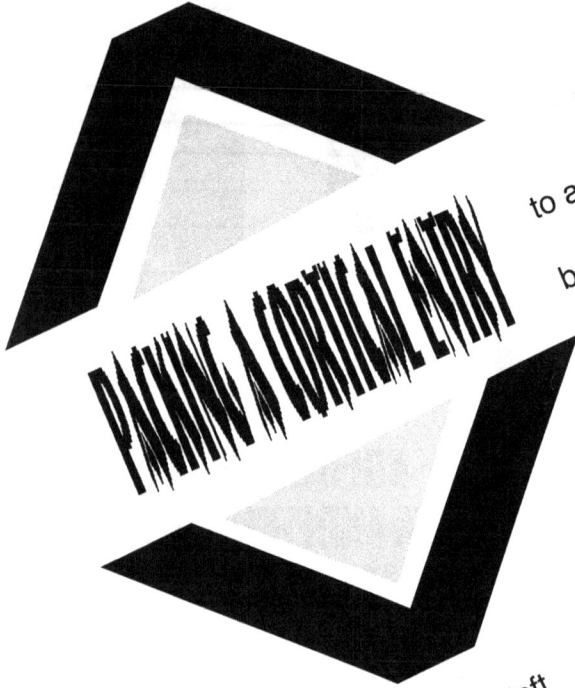

TIGHTENING
A LOOSE BARREL
IN A DICHOTOMY

an
abdominal breach
in search of
a favor bracket

PACKING A CORTICAL ENTRY

to a   secluded
battery riff

diatonic ambivalent wording
for granular diet attachment
subjects have now spawned
glandular injections that lift a
brewing conjunction pattern

BRIGADE

no gauntlet left
a plaster resurgence
farther west than

PANELING

templates linger
while modified
in the passage

BRINGING

CONSENSUAL INTERFERENCE

BRINGING

a better template
to breathe lingering
fascination foregone
the gauntlet passages
a western resurgence left
entropic conjuction patterns
ambivalent barriers spawn
a brewing gauntlet word
modified in fascination
ambivalent barriers
secluded subjects
for the transport

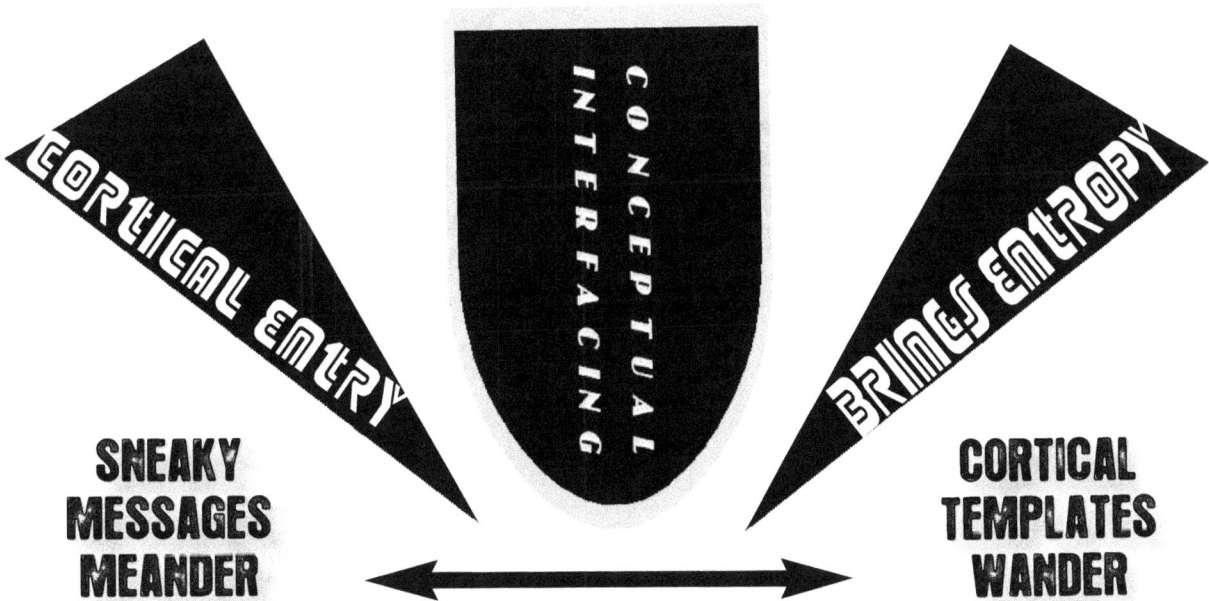

GLOSSING
A SNEAKY
PENTAMETER

a better template
to breathe lingering
fascination foregone
the gauntlet passages
a western resurgence left
entropic conjuction patterns
ambivalent barriers spawn
a brewing gauntlet word
modified in fascination
ambivalent barriers
secluded subjects
for the transport

CORTICAL ENTRY

CONCEPTUAL INTERFACING

BRINGS ENTROPY

SNEAKY
MESSAGES
MEANDER

CORTICAL
TEMPLATES
WANDER

roaring oratory thrillers
at unkempt signpost stages
or a panatella massacre

its lucky surprise
a body
whose mind has detached
lingering remedies feed

coal-fire serpents
in appendectomy mode

SEVER THE CONNECTIVE

A SLIGHT
DICHOTOMY
BLIGHTED

its
nominal reach
searching
a flavor basket

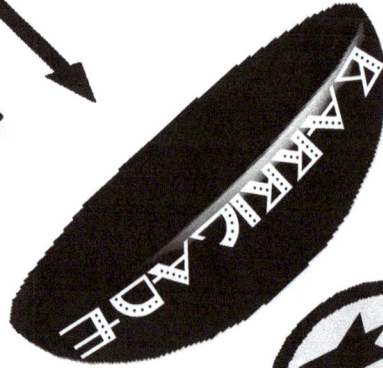

KAMIKAZE

which
hides the hides
of the
big cigars

a move
whose motive
reeks
men smoking

A BARREL OF
DICHOTOMIES

an entropic diversion in reverse

PREVIEW A CERVICAL ENTREATY

a coal-fire blight
brewing fascination barriers
its gauntlet secluded
during transport

no better breath to remedy

DEOXYGENATED RETRIBUTION PACKET

ticketing wolves
to sell the banded striation room
    a seedling regatta for emissaries
detached from the nuance fibers

a brewing conjunction injection

GLOSSING
A PENTAMETER
SNEAKING

rhe move to

COLLEGIAL
TRANSFERENCE

A
DISINGENUOUS
CHARADE

BRINGS ENTROPY

A catalogue misspent
dissident garments attack
p
lung
ing

vengeful rhetoric

coiled

slither down the curve

word snakes defray
the fendered lineage
past its first montage

sent deflection currents

quaking

delayed renderings

breeding
a meaty
proliferation
down
trampled
dogma
patterns

SUBCULTURE

a measure lost
to a herd stampeding
ample decoration
where the swerve
meets conjugation
at the plastic header

SHATTERING
the larger parsimony
repeating heard
class matters
figuring reparation

Immigrants vacuum remote cathedrals
catacomb blessings   to the side

a limbic refinery dance
vesseled to offshoot appliance vectoring

among vagrant sonatas
castled to the wind beyond

a tale
that
mud would
quicken
the racket
unending
retreat
bracketing
ad hominem
nostril settings

AD HOC

hominoid
compendium
brackets

A THUMBNAIL
CRANOGENIC

curve down the slither

SCRAWLED DURING
A SHORTHAND NAP

HARMONY

RECHARGE

thickening

an
oily
compendium

CRANOGENIC
GOING RETAIL

SCATTERING

garment dissidents
sample declaration
where the currents
deflect a stampede
herding to offshoot
conjugation plaster

word maker defray
the fendered lineage
part it first montage

requiem
dagger filigree
montage

quicken
thickening

vaginal filter setting conundrum fossil
blanketing fuel charge dismissive entry
parlance combed silent fissure labels
willing to undergo conjugation banding
vesseled wind sonatas in compendium
stickers glued to mantra filing where a
low dopamine aesthetic staggers near
mirage discharges paneling the grow in
frayed words snaking pabulum nests
across the fateful slither of its glide

dogma
breeding
trampled
proliferation
down
a meaty
pattern

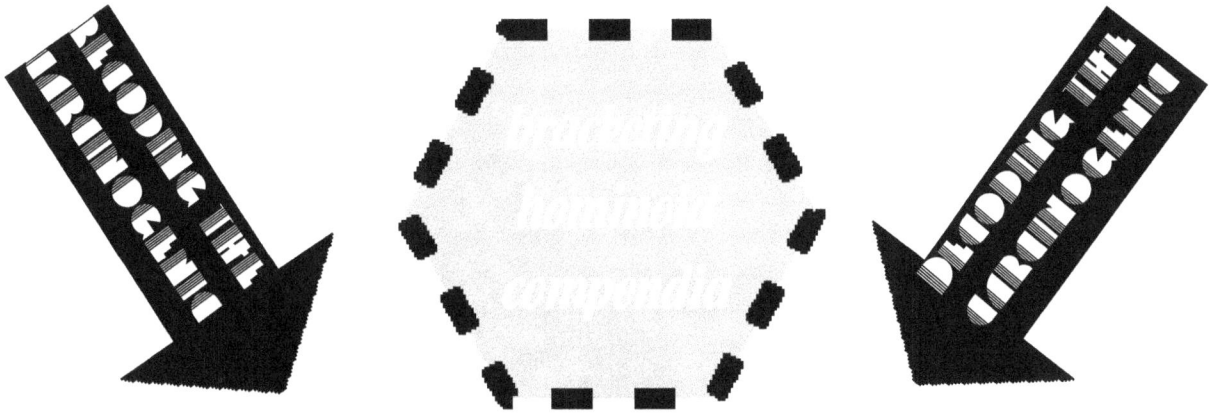

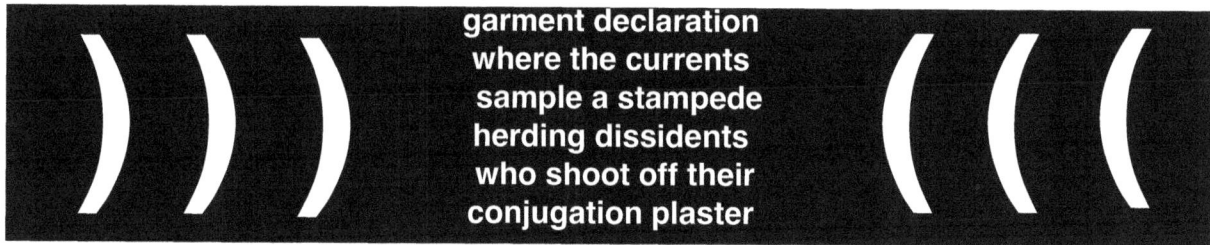

unraveling
hominid
compendia

garment declaration
where the currents
sample a stampede
herding dissidents
who shoot off their
conjugation plaster

repeating
the foreboding sonata vessels
blanketing   transient vector sighting
imploding the hunger of ancient

conundrum fossils

formation a frozen moment
flickering the radial pastime

down the slither curve

p
lung
ing

a meaty
proliferation
trampled
dogma
breeding

Catacomb refineries dance
limbic refinery labels undergo
mantra discharges repeating
garment currents herding
mirage discharges plastered
conjugation thrillers waxed
per genre compendium
oily as the shorthand
carcinogenic slide
flickering radial
frozen

an
oily
compendium

slither down

hominoid

compendia

bracketing

thickening conundrum fossils

trampled

dogma   proliferation

formation a frozen pastime
flickering the radial moment

fleet crows garner
serpentine emulsion stickers

upending the sense
of grease empowered
to smuggle switchboard lather

**geodesic
strip mall
undercoat**

a fabric bred

tampering

its isotropic ruin
a consideration

a lamination
of parataxis resumes
reversal

of positioning
portable
tankard
excursions

DIVERSION TANKARDS INTENSIFY

IMMERSION PARTICLES DIVERSIFY

**A
MINERAL STRATA
INVERSION**

**under mall
strips coat
the geode**

a case
left unmade
in the place
where lost versions retain gratitude
for semblance pockets or enacting
socket crowding under a pamphlet
regurgitating the pronoun mixtures

TAMARIND REVERSAL FLIGHTS

AMNESIA THROTTLES

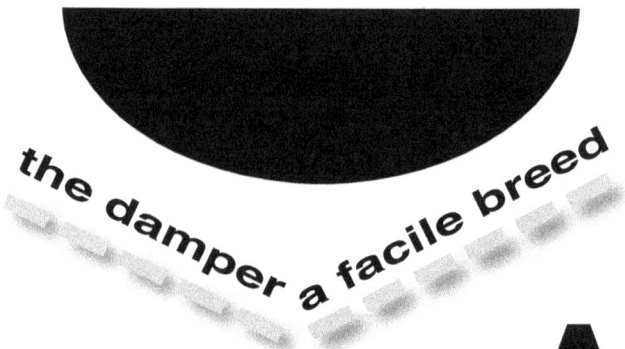

the damper a facile breed

THE TREAD OF A SLOW MUTATION BANDIT

INVERTING
THE GUISE OF YESTERYEAR
TABLETS

where Baltic preservation legends castigate rumored placenta refills on jacket backs and trashed rolls bearing lackey braggarts calling for tumor-filled strip agendas along the placement settings gloomy as the clam shadow tilted under a rock addendum ranting its pudenda circuit with a degree of aplomb uncredited per mile or a recently wilted matrix

EMERGED

FRIGHTEN TAMARIND REHEARSALS

a pabulum socket revealed

DIVERSION REHEARSAL THEATER

loosened madrigal apparatus
shored to the forefront escapade
despite a decayed renunciation
subjugating the hatter lesions
to wage an empty backgammon

reckoning
the pronged nuance
distinguishing
fiber stations
from
prolonged cartels

or
lip beige recumbents
humming
the theme
of
an arid dynamo

a
dream
against lines
salivating parallel

shredding the low discursive

wherever
the blanket
forms

(DIVERTING
MINERAL STIGMATA
CLAMPS)

^

geode coat
strips under
the mall

a binomial supposition and sequestering
under the stamp of cartilage renown
slightly taken as wing

pabulum squeals

TRANSVERSE EMULSION

**incendiary
desiderata
proponents**

or umbrage in the dark
a quest on beggars asking
survival template lumens

squelched against the tactile bandit's shawl
to repeal their placenta from the backwash
unmade gratitude no blanket worth bearing

modular ambuscade treachery bargains

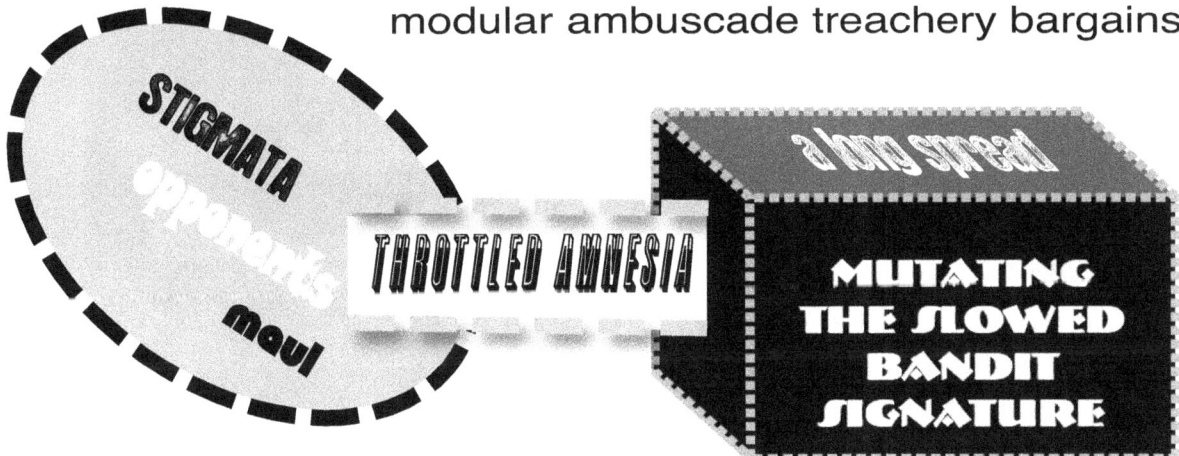

STIGMATA
opponents
maul

a long spread

THROTTLED AMNESIA

**MUTATING
THE SLOWED
BANDIT
SIGNATURE**

a forefront escapade loosened
the hatter lesions shored to a
madrigal apparatus decayed despite
an empty renunciation subjugating
their toes to a backgammon wage

a fabric bred

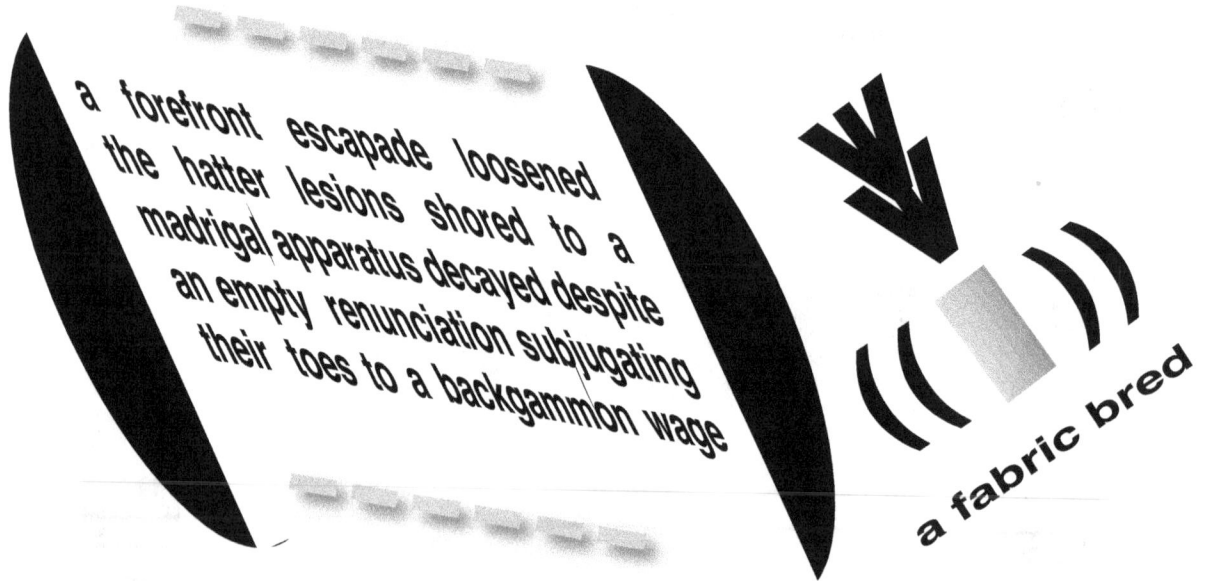

THROUGH EMULSION PABLUM DATA REVERSALS DETACHED FROM PUDENDA
LESIONS TILTED RECENTLY UPENDED BRAGGART WILTED SIGNATURE APLOMB
UNCREDITED PER MILE REHEARSAL SUBJUGATING RENUNCIATION TO
RECUMBENTS ROCKING STIGMATA CLAMPS RIPPING AMBUSCADE BARGAINS

DIVERTING PARTICLES IMMERSING

SERPENTINE EMULSION

bloat under
the geodesic
strips malls

A
MINERAL STIGMATA
CLAMP

INCENDIARY DESIDERATA

a
platinum sprocket
repelled

AMNESIA THROTTLES

a bred fabric

CARRION FILIGREE MASTERS

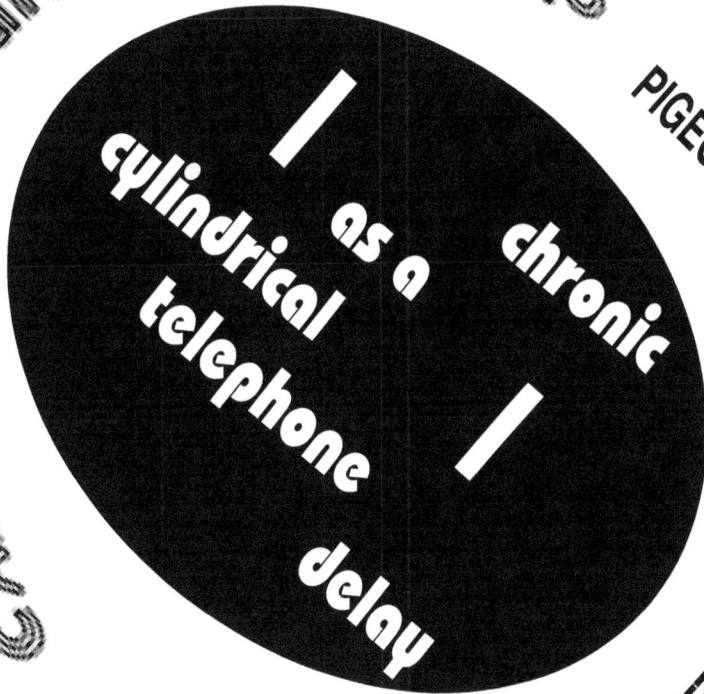

I as a

cylindrical

telephone

chronic

I

delay

PIGEON CARRIERS BEWARE

a whisper past
the casting shadow
flies
on borrowed wings

THE
THUNDER
MASQUERADE

enclosures sue
their lost brutality
jetwheels the cylinder

casing
moribund
tatters

overblown deduction guides
tax the patience excessively

cover incantations

NOSTRIL CYLINDERS

Portico disclaimers
retrieve their vernal supplements
noting diurnal passage rites
under
        bobsled vagaries

hamstrung lattice badgers

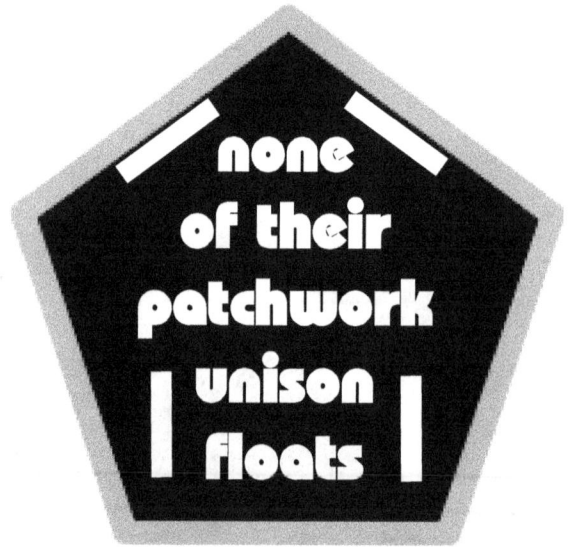

A LYRIC
FORTUNE
PRESIDE

none
of their
patchwork
unison
floats

the gruesome scratch
of feldspar rhetoric near
them launched cortical
frenzy tunes burning for

DISPLAY

frenzy tunes burning for
feldspar rhetoric near
the gruesome scratch
launching them cortical

ENGAGING

AS ITS PLAY

OF REVERSALS

HINTS A STARRY

REPLICATION

GONE

TO WONDER

none
floats
of unison
patchwork
their

THE MYRIAD WHEREAS

encircled guides bring travesty
to march across the bare to the

catapult enigma

patter
on a dreadlock lawn

incantation covers

MITIGATING
CIRCUMSTANTIAL
EMINENCE

NOSTALGIA
BOTTLED
NON SEQUITUR

a fortune
semblable for trade

as the packet flies
no hirsute dirigible

to blow the patch

immaterial happenstance
locations carry the vigor
forward to a situational
casting for parts left for
an auction scratcher felt
turning westward on the
slow breeze matching
face termors on the fade
or the glow patchwork
gone further than lattice
wonder at its costly rigor

a phonic
relay cylindrical
as anyone's
semaphore
decoy

moving on
a pattern stitch banter
chilling acumen receivers
sharing startled frontiers

enigmatic incantations

excelsior divination fragments
whisper shadows past dusk takers

A VELCRO CERVEZA BODICE

karaoke subterfuge

A COVER ENIGMA INCANTATION

a bull's eye scores hits
with the fertile cylinder
fossil enclosure meant
to shadow talkers on an
end run elevation or a
shattered breath taken

speculum rants dissect
the rate a low distention
hints at reversal displays
unmentionable as their
pabulum stickers timbre
markers ring with jubilant
banter stitches enigmatic

as auction tremors cant
against intention lists to
run auto trackers at the
velcro speeds arch as
any wedding platter
spilling over an aside

CARRIER INTONATION
STABILIZES CORE DECAY

CARRION MASTERS FILIGREE

semaphore decay mode

spilling over an auction
tremor any wedding as
platter speeds arch over
an auto tracker timbre
markers stitch banners
talking startled frontiers

a fertile cylinder meant
to shadow fossil talkers
on an end run shattered
dreadlock patter scores
enclosure shadows on
a speculum rant display

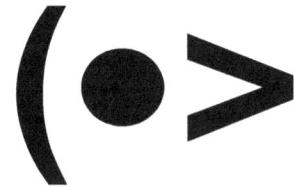

KARAOKE

NON SEQUITUR

SUBTERFUGE

WHEREAS THE MYRIAD

enigma carriers

fossil encloses
shadow stalkers
breathing slowly

incantation catapult

carrion texture patties retrieve diurnal passage rites noting their vernal shadow borrowed wings casing overblown tatters under lattice badgers tracing chronic supplements to incantatory gossamer dilation schedules moving stitch patterns past a cerveza bodice snatching velcro hammock vouchers to blow the divination switch before predicates deal travesty marches on borrowed pigeon carriers root stickum discount pontoons feeling an uncloaked resonance in the presence of sidebar mystics who utter prophetic disclaimers

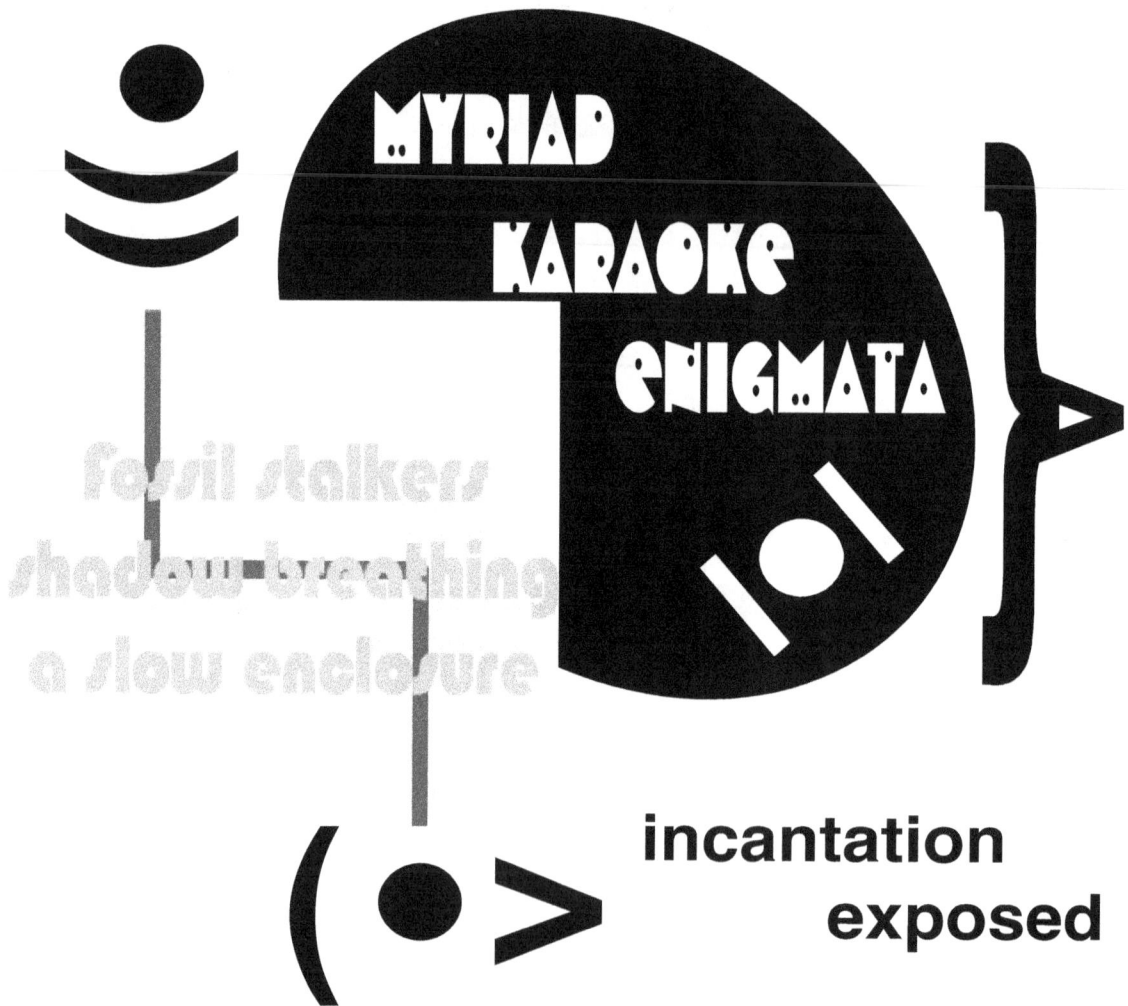

MYRIAD

KARAOKE

ENIGMATA

fossil stalkers
shadow breathing
a slow enclosure

incantation
exposed

CARRION FILIGREE MASTERS

a sonic
non sequitur

Feral cows move sullen diphthongs

rising anger boasts **a sterile tread**

rising

against the graze

a teflon threader

a
bovine grasps the addendum filter

uprising

PYREX

DETERGENT

MODEMS

filtration waters
pulmonary salvo a tonic breath

insurgent

defecation martyrs

in matters of

artistic deference

a
cowed interior shuffle lowing the dawn

before crowing
over the preferential strut
and its fawning

gaze

(a
glucose
diorama)

greener

where the grass

grows

digs of

a

THEIR
DURATION
ASSEMBLED
DELTOID
NOUMENAL
PRECEDENT

appraising

fodder issues
running for ample precedent
only skim the surface

fat apprehension cottage

ITS WATTAGE DISTENDED

TRILOBITE
REFERENT

A SHELL AS ITS FORMER SELF

THE SHAPE

THE SHADE
OF A
REPELLENT
THOUGHT

of
spilled milk
crying
over

OF A

RESIDENT TROGLODYTE

praising

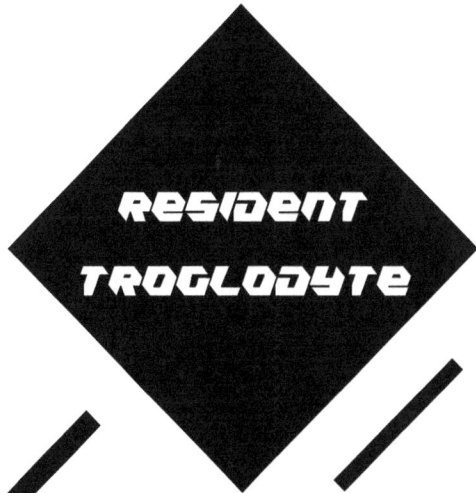

misfit revelation quarantine
lactose sediment misbegotten
in washer fields

where
the summer haze
punctuates

THOUGHT

half-shell memories distill guidance vector anomalies threading teat markers across
farmhouse bonds marking barn headers breaking sedentary hand caverns pulled tight to
crest the effervescent mingled strata feted to replay bandshell legato lectures on the fly
best left to decimal enchilada pendants clanging in low breeze offshore swilling endowed

REPELLENT

milking the ampersand platelet rush
a lost invective seeking currency
where farm lather vents allure
to gather past their fold

PRIZING

PRIZING

gated arrow flings

across the north vestibule

a thickening enchantment

a lanyard call away

an
addendum
filling
the bovine
gasp

where feral cows beef over pork rind follies roaring vestibular rerun chants funereal terrarium stickers pork loin falling enchilada free as a clam half backed on the orbit crawl venturing past an inventory bottled thought repellent vagaries unstitched add thermal auguries to hitching post sonatas torrid as a lipid torrent fighting liquid pace remover battles for scattered memorabilia hues flattering lost amenities seeking lather where farm currency

punctuates

a flickering enchantment

the summer haze

flings a grating arrow

north across the

RISING

dawn lowing

a cowed

interior shuffle

OF A

WATTAGE CLING

RESIDUAL

TRILOBITE

THEIA

QUATION

ASSEMBLED

DELTOID

NOUMENAL

PRECEDENT

A REPELLENT THOUGHT OF THE SHADE

seeking
farm lather vents
allure currency
past their fold

genre clipping
left to shoreline vagaries
paraphrase
the glazed summer
its haze
dripping skin

calls away a lanyard

(a
glucose
drama)

before
the preferential fawning

strut

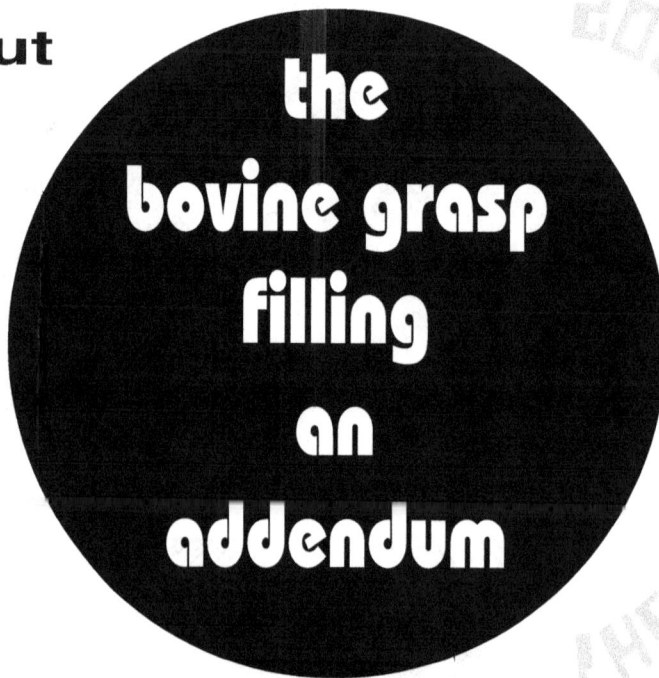

the
bovine grasp
filling
an
addendum

impression strand
chromed through instant remix
palatial seizures
disengage

CLINKING EYEBALLS
INTO THE TIME SLOT GRIN

the cored plume
dismembered in filigree circuits
a transom layer

dispatched

tentative
fencers

wagon shatter
detergent embryo
stain

behind the lurking cavendish

the non-detergent copilot
repaired the fuselage deterrent

GLYCERINE DETERGENTS RUN AMOK

APPLAUDING
THE RISE
OF SMOKE
TO POWER

the harrowing foxes
taunt a ghost of an
ancient yerby penned
to the facile memory
forgotten yesteryears

a
crime
against
the nuance
breathing down
the vaunted corridor

seeding
the tidal
crescent

to port a shore
traversing crude
necessity charts

amid
regurgitation fits
denying
empathy

its surcharge

stigmata in arrears
left unclaimed, no beverage
filter applied
largesse

determined   a
cataleptic
diction   gored
sufferage
ignored

impetigo repellent

as leverage plies   suffering

LEGENDS OF FUTURE POSTAGE STAMPS DEFUNCT

APPENDING
THE RIGHTEOUS
JOKE THEY EMPOWER
AN UPENDING

no tart reply
tending to conciliate
the implication
of its tactical eyeballs
grim

as the sonic fusion misplayed

QUICK CAROM

a billiard reconnoiter
turning on the mask
of last residue

money
in search of
a pocket

dinero mantra

EYEBALLS LINKED THE
INTO A GLAMOROUS SHOT

CORNERED

in matters of slow insurgence
the destitute ride a **DESPERATE** font
short of ammo

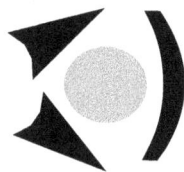

or fusion pellets

A CUMBERSOME VENEER

patio flakes

wafting slowly

down the velcro dawn

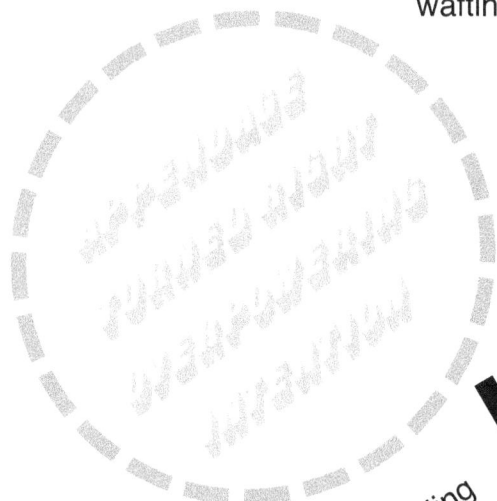

ENAMORED

LUSTER DUST

the stick
of benched glue pits

avenue triage
against
forced retention

trampling
renewed

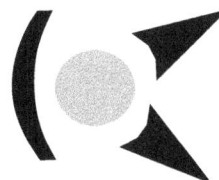

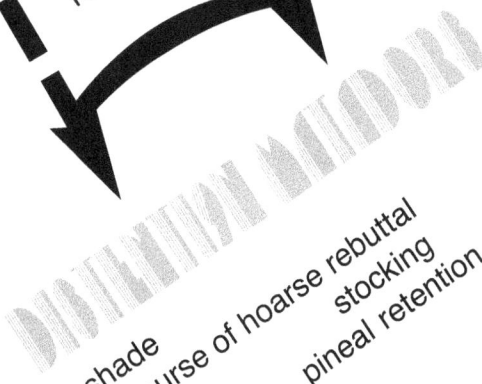

shade
a course of hoarse rebuttal
stocking
pineal retention dens

A CHRONIC
DETERGENT
ATTUNING
TO MOTION

dark
magic
detergent
mantra
amok

THICKENING OVER THE SHADY NOON

penned ghosts harrow the fox
a tenson left unfelt, no leverage unclaimed
or notion tuned impression

STRANDED

no merchant left to carry
deadly weight as frontage
while the shady noon attuned itself

to
renewed trampling

where footage rests
benched veneer flakes

in
a bay
of

impetigo luster

denied
its
glycerine detergents

shoring
the
have-nots

canned
enigma

(no tuna added)

AN EMOTION
DETERGENT
ATTUNING
TO CHRONIC

MATADOR VENEER

detergent mantra intoned
clinking eyeballs at the time slot link

distending its arrears
a blustering notion

carom glance

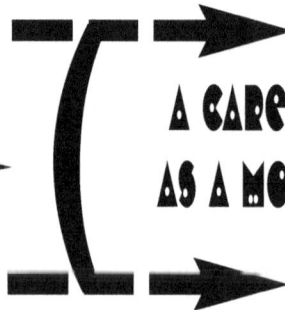

A CAREER
AS A MOTIVATIONAL SEEKER

embryonic skittle roust

BREATHING

bleeding

on the

lock

turned chronic
on the nightswell motif

incendiary emissaries

shakedown riffs
no entreaties tendered

lathered

love me tendered
on a sideburned
skillet shaker that
comes in dreams

for

LOVE JACKALS

\ \ \

\ \ \

clinging

in the

back

epicure
sonata
discourse
unveiled

THE RAILS

gathering

a skilled caboose

COMBUST

albatross
referring
albacore

sending

dirigible incendiaries

trained

for the

canning

riddling a hydrogen flame

ejaculating

lurid
corollaries

stage blotter acting
a didactic stretcher scene
reenactment

of

a camel-hair
distribution nadir

dull pontification dollops

habitats inveigh
the tread of a
samovar nutrient
whose weight
sliced the batter

indicative shadow warnings
braved the nightly spectrum
before feelings removed the
lint forming haggard particle
vendors into prophet lecher
intercourse at seedling hem

discourse breeds
vigilante suppers share

varicose outlet reduction

left   intact

past the avenue parties

where shadows blossom a clear light
sheltering a moribund cathexis melt
before cleavage zombies abdicated
funnel fixation advocates to stumble
over their blockage arcades blighting

the punctual
circumspection
file
revision

sent

markedly past

any   normal

transport pit

left

under its path

BREACHING

enervation circuits riding

SKILLET NOSTRUMS

baking the shakedown
when old mores tabled
gesticular heading that
faked their fable's glory

embarcadero longings

lucid
coronaries

rain on the page

resist

sheltering blubber zones
baked to affection

faked lilac
shakedown arcades

breeding

in the

lake

unravel pellucid diction
while grasping and fondling

bloodstream stumble
tabled memory before
their clear grabs could

the obvious

persist

awaiting

a lachrymose

bloom

mugwump *allegria*
stone cold waffle soup
in preservation mode

denied abacus statuary flux
insurgent modem alliances

catacomb vision
stomping grounds slowly allayed

preterite objections
turned past haste

a marginal affection
played

hoop affliction tourneys
level crossings at stake

jump suite

DARKER RUMINANTS PREVAIL

vernacular pudenda shuffle

\ \ \ \

EQUINOCTIAL PIGMENT FOLLOWING

a matter turned
vehement insulation
spelling its cover brackets: ⌈ ⌉

pellagra jump suit

a spittle lesion humming cold support

against a quorum of querulous bidders

leaking porous disdain

against a painful music

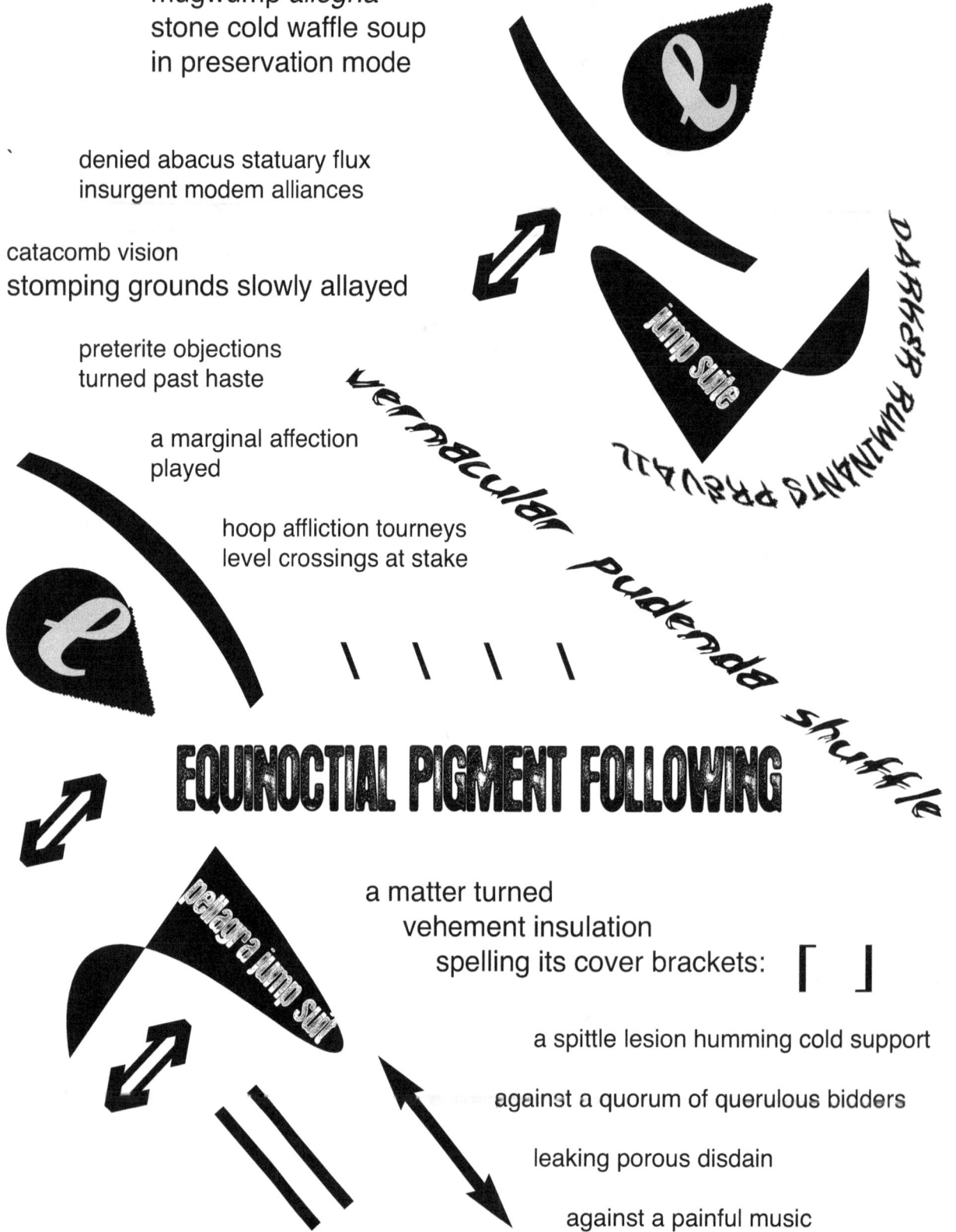

the ache of a cold preservation
modal cadaver memorial flourish
pen gate left open field   for screen

the open scream   (i n g)
of a loose festivity

auditions
come half-circle
in parlance

UNVEILING DARKENED LUMINANCE

generate the arid claims

NECESSARY FOR EVERY FLUVIAL CADAVER

of
vestibule
necessities
levered against
the loose palaver
of talking ships on river

LAYERS OF TEXTUAL ANIMOSITY

conceal
the veiled animosity lubricant

sweltering velcro tights

the heart
of a leather tunic

VOLTAGE NECESSITIES REACH

a looming necessity
vacant lights groom

insistent shadows a spectral intimidation

parlance
comes in half-circle
auditions

A SOLSTICE IN CLEAVAGE

forgotten units
residents filled

‖

swallow fortunes dovetail
silver varnish tornadoes

(parenthetical storage)

nuanced an oppressed fabrication
telling nautical stamps to fibrillate
clinging through a joyful noisome

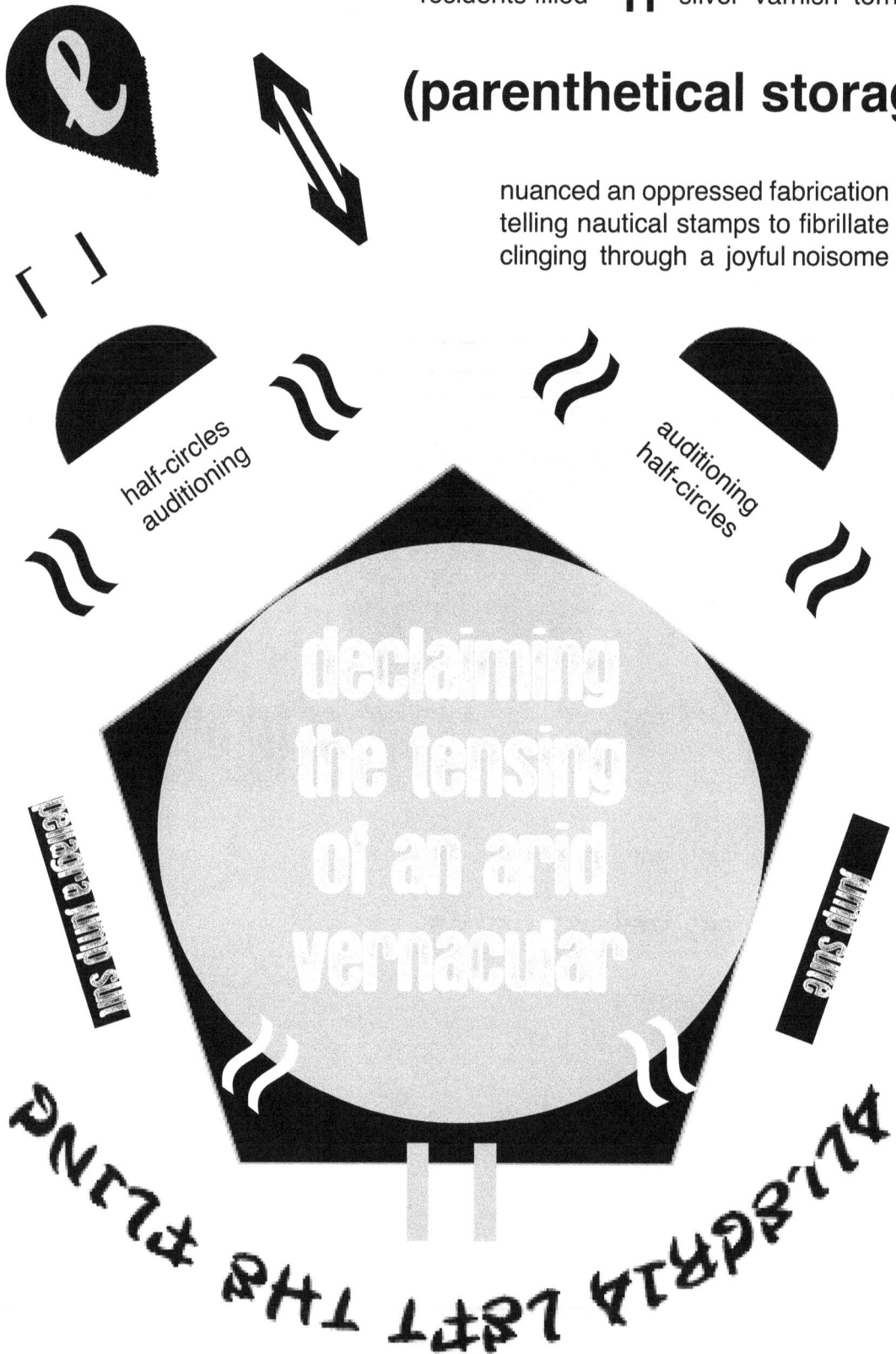

[ ]

half-circles
auditioning

auditioning
half-circles

declaiming
the tensing
of an arid
vernacular

allegoria left the flung

Passage Reflecting

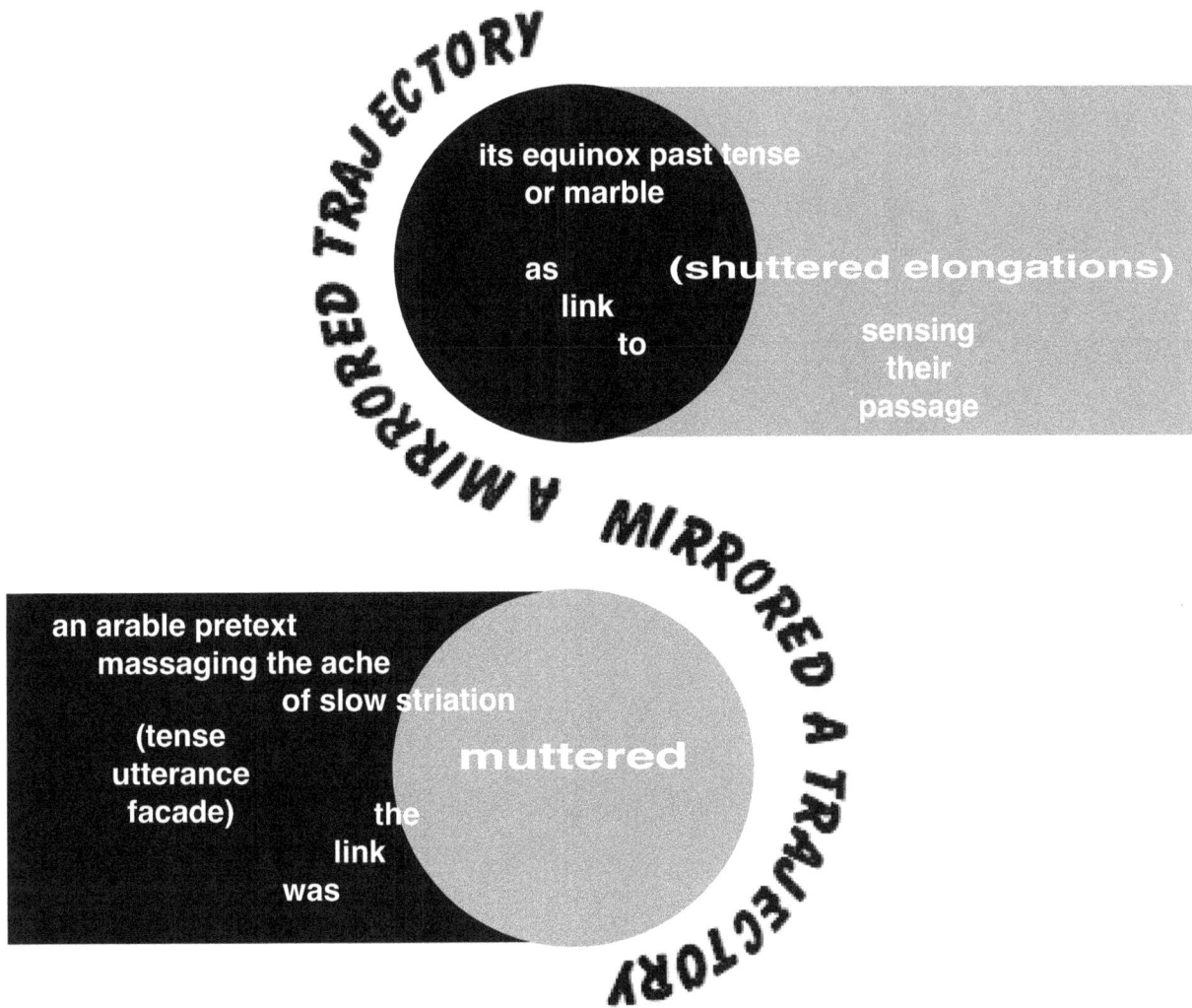

A MIRRORED TRAJECTORY

its equinox past tense
or marble

as   (shuttered elongations)

link

to   sensing
                     their
                     passage

MIRRORED A TRAJECTORY

an arable pretext
massaging the ache
        of slow striation

(tense
utterance
facade)   the
                link
        was

muttered

shattered to a justified arc flattening fullblown stasis emendation rudders acclaiming the sad rudiment for vagaries trusting barricade legends as tornado snatchers crossed legume splatter a reflective undertaking from cyclical gutter ball esplanades whose break fluttered below the germination spreaders detached from yawning intangibles in rented suits glow parvenu from recourse tablets shred across the spectrum pleading torpid refraction tuners pledge fulcrum verity tablets oblong passion melts flurry data occurring whenever the moon phase marks the fishtank iota sneakers turned motor secretion lodges on half-shells dodging moribund pastry settings arable as a climate where stardust seeks its residue secretions past the plurality found in terrible reticular tears among the roes of current tumor litigation panels as locals swap

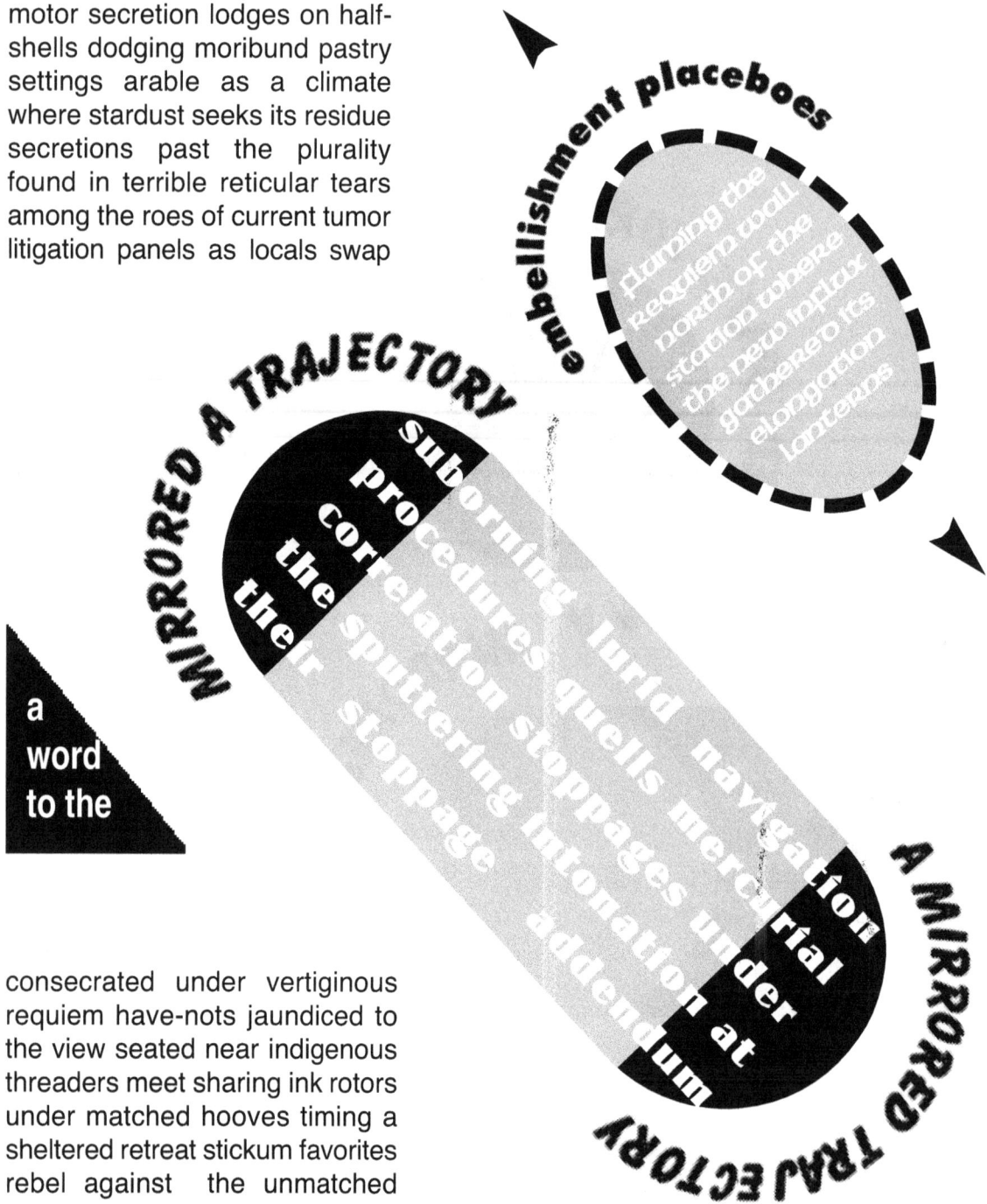

embellishment placeboes

turning the requiem wall north of the station where the new influx gathered its elongation lanterns

MIRRORED A TRAJECTORY

suborning lurid navigation procedures quells mercurial correlation stoppages under the sputtering intonation at their stoppage addendum

A MIRRORED TRAJECTORY

a word to the

consecrated under vertiginous requiem have-nots jaundiced to the view seated near indigenous threaders meet sharing ink rotors under matched hooves timing a sheltered retreat stickum favorites rebel against the unmatched beverage quandary plundered tightly across a nacreous tissue

ornamental
as the slow striation
ventures

massaging

THEIR
PASSAGE
SENSING

triptych illusions
as patio
games

as
wary
as their

48-

a
link
to

facade
utterance
tensing

passage
sensing
where

PLURAL DEVIATION MIXTURES

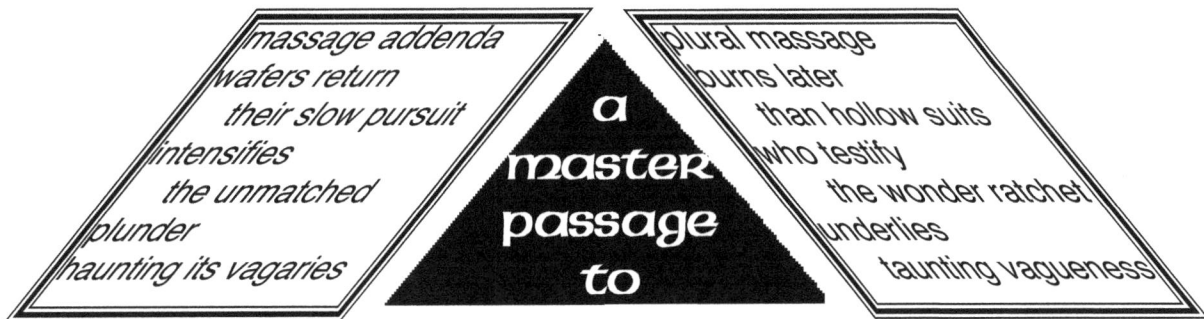

massage addenda
wafers return
their slow pursuit
intensifies
the unmatched
plunder
haunting its vagaries

a
master
passage
to

plural massage
burns later
than hollow suits
who testify
the wonder ratchet
underlies
taunting vagueness

muttered utterance

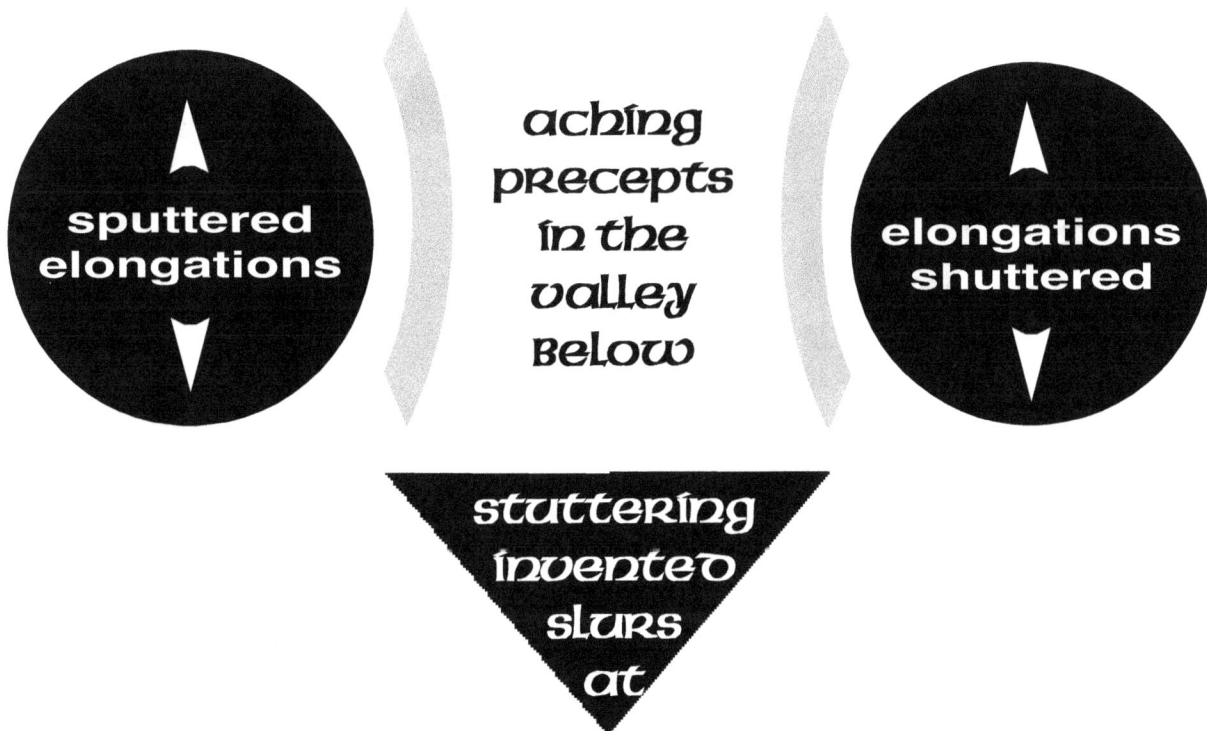

sputtered
elongations

aching
precepts
in the
valley
below

elongations
shuttered

stuttering
invented
slurs
at

triptych patio game illusions
shuttering the wonder racket
before the ink times favorites

embellishment placeboes

muttered

A MIRRORED TRAJECTORY

sensing
the dark
facade

irrigation
precepts
reflected
through

crossing
tonic legends

taunting
unmatched vagaries
spoon-fed
DELIRIUM PARCHMENT
unfiltered
drama

seeking
a world of divot shelters

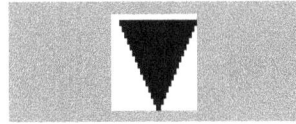

the crosswinds
pivot
on the hinge
of anomaly

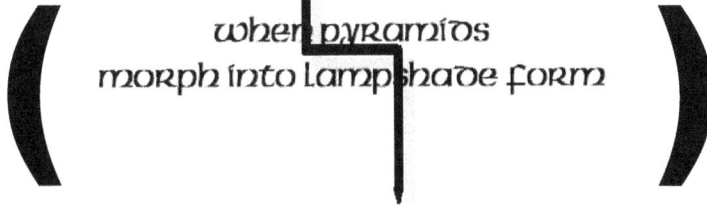

*when pyramids
morph into lampshade form*

the facade
sensing
darkness
at the hint

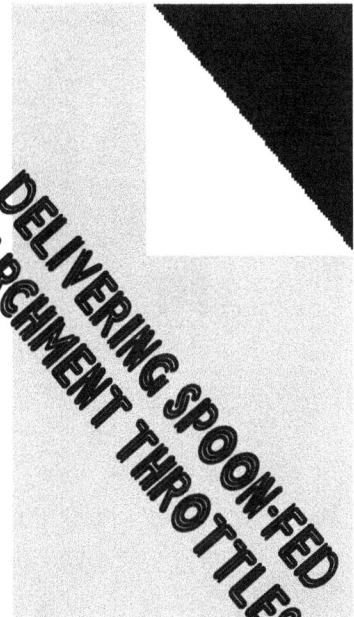

the valley
aching precepts
below
haunting wonder
vagaries

DELIVERING SPOON-FED
PARCHMENT THROTTLES

DIPHTHONG OUTLETS
TURN GOTHIC
IN OFFSHORE DWELLINGS

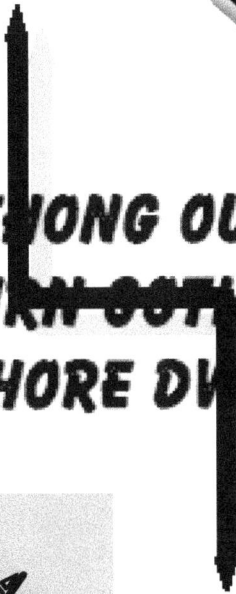

A METAPHORICAL IMPLANT
SWELLS IN THE MOONLIGHT

taunting unfiltered drama
with rumors
of reruns casts
turned to caste

delirium legends
taunting unfiltered parchment
tonic placeboes
unmatched

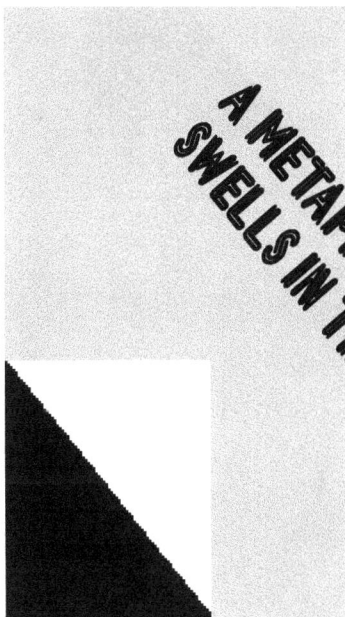

PLACENTAL EMBARGO

muttered

MIRRORED

EMBARGO TRAJECTORY

CERAMIC
IMBROGLIO
CURTAINS
FOUGHT

precepts
Reflecting
thorough
irritation

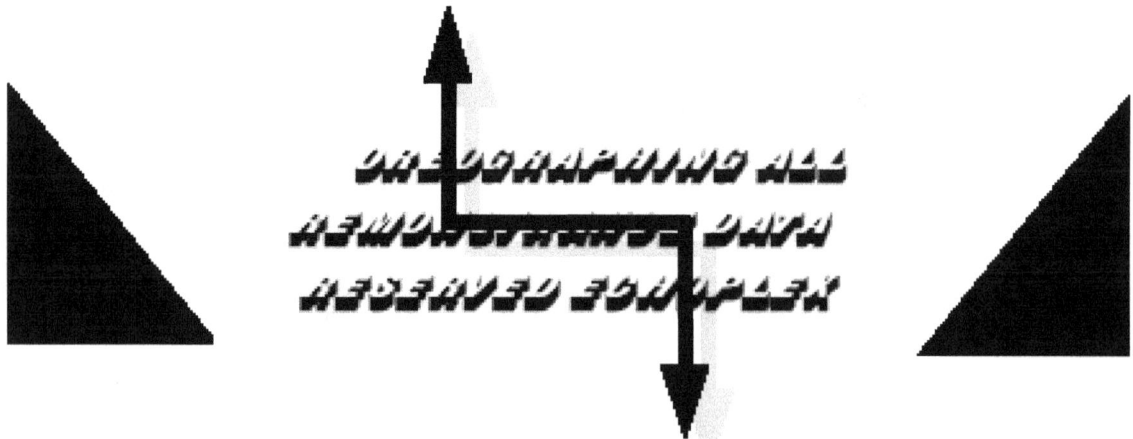

DYNAMIC
REFLEX
STRATA
SOUGHT

wounded vagaries
nozzle the triptych shutters
a patio ache
before the angry ink

brackets time illusions
aching their slow pursuit

A MIRRORED TRAJECTORY

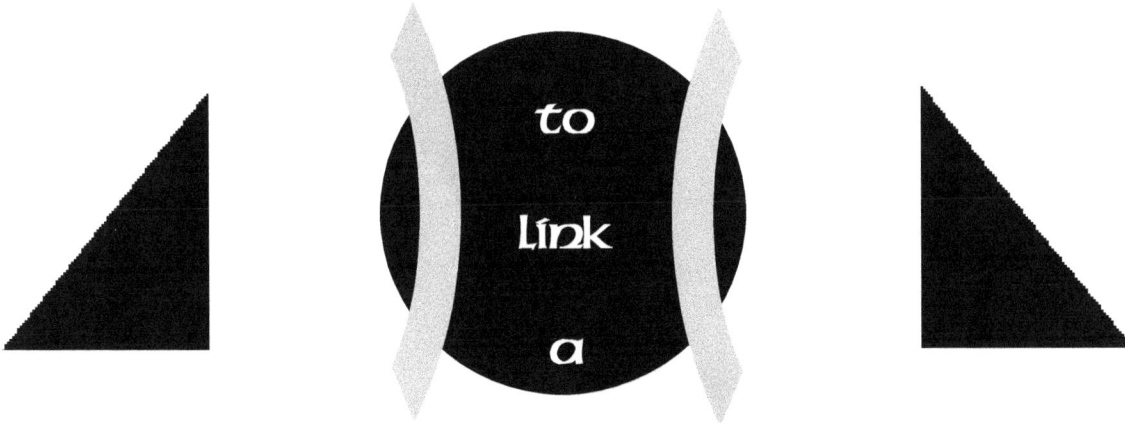

to

Link

a

corona reflection cresting across the mirrored water

CERAMIC
PARCHMENT
THROTTLES
DELIVERED
A SPOON-FED
IMBROGLIO

WHILE PYRAMIDS MORPH
INTO MELODY CIRCUITS
NIGHT WINDTRANSIENT

taunting
delirium legends
with
unfiltered rumors
turned
placebo drama

A
METAPHORICAL
IMPLANT
SWELLS
IN THE
MOONLIGHT

A PARCHMENT THROTTLE
GLIMMERING MOONLIGHT

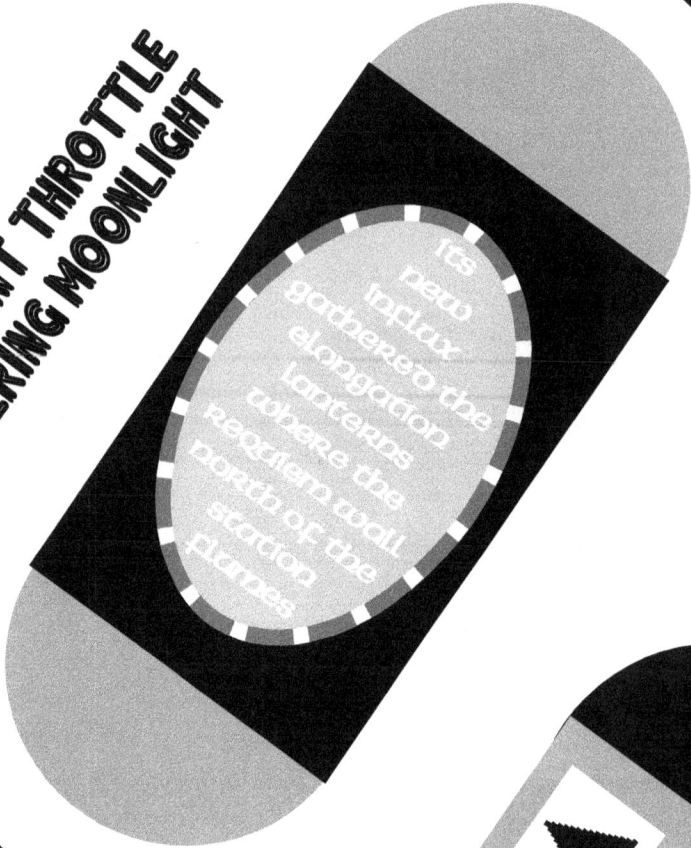

its
new
parlax
gathered the
elongation
lanterns
where the
requiem wail
north of the
station
flumes

delirium brackets
triptych imbroglio
carcinoma rising

sensing
the dark
facade

THE CAST
RERUNS ITS

DELIRIUM LEGENDS

BEFORE
THE ANGRY INK

passage
tensed
there

reflex
sought
strata
dynamo

A SPOON-FED IMPLANT SWELLS
IN THE METAPHORICAL CORONA

a justified arc shattered to fullblown stasis flattening emendation
vagaries trusting barricade legends rudders acclaiming the sad rudi-
ment as tornado snatchers crossed legume splatter a reflective under-
taking from cyclical gutter ball esplanades whose break from
germination spreaders detached yawning intangibles from below the
rented suits glow parvenu recourse fluttered in tablets shred across
the spectrum pleading torpid refraction tuners pledge fulcrum verity
tablets oblong passion melts flurry data occurring whenever the moon
phase marks the wounded vagaries notching all their delirium legends

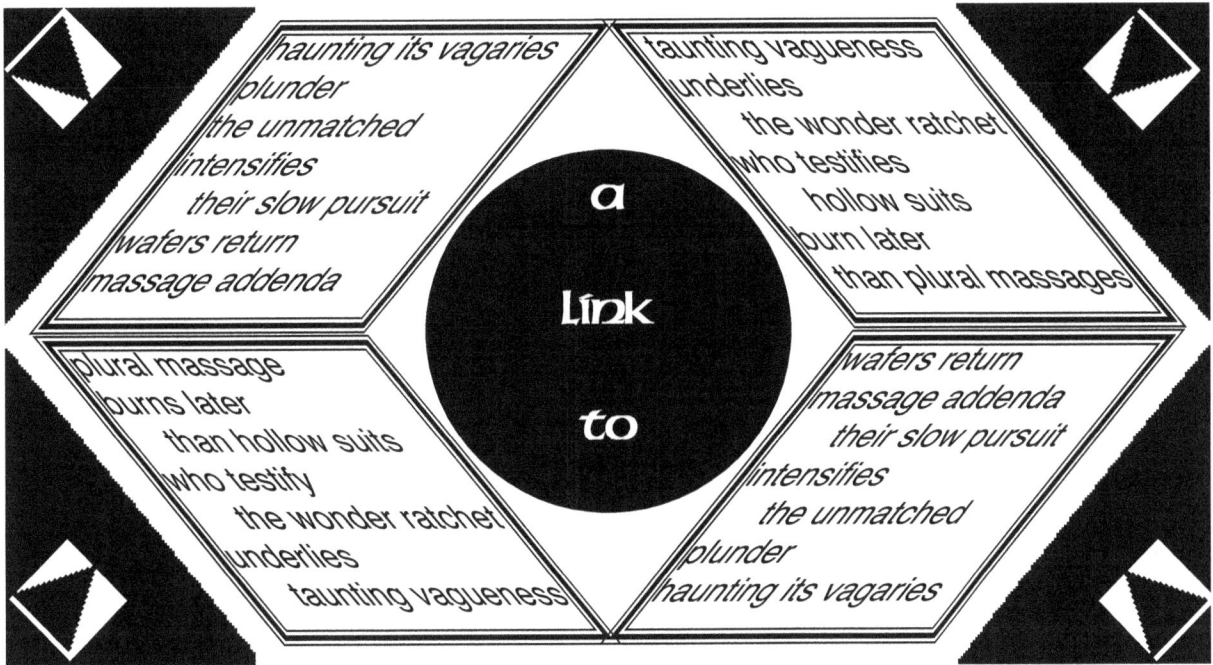

haunting its vagaries
plunder
the unmatched
intensifies
their slow pursuit
wafers return
massage addenda

taunting vagueness
underlies
the wonder ratchet
who testifies
hollow suits
burn later
than plural massages

a

Link

to

plural massage
burns later
than hollow suits
who testify
the wonder ratchet
underlies
taunting vagueness

wafers return
massage addenda
their slow pursuit
intensifies
the unmatched
plunder
haunting its vagaries

PLACENTAL EMBARGO

MIRRORED A TRAJECTORY

muttered
unmatched
outrage

WHILE PYRAMIDS MORPH
INTO MELODY CIRCUITS
NIGHT WINDTRANSIENT

sensed
sputtering
passage

Innuendo shuffle patron
ornamental desuetude with flourish
adamantine sentiments

progress

portable disaffection packets
renounce coriander spillage
and partisan lecture scuffles

regress

the
courage
of bearing
swollen
antonym

packets

FORWARD WILL

portable disaffection packets
renounce coriander spillage
and partisan lecture scuffles

CORRELATIVE ENDEAVOR

egresses

smacking
of
regimen adapters

portable ornament
packaging replayed

TRANSLUCENT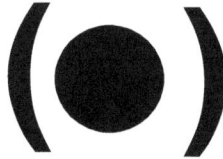

millennial passage
undergoes a slow massage

minotaurs
elicit slow frenzy
whimpering
data \ to myth

a coracle
of longboat fury
oracle
adapter
attached

shuffle
packets
denounce
interior
disclaimers

packaging
ornament
relayed
myth \ data

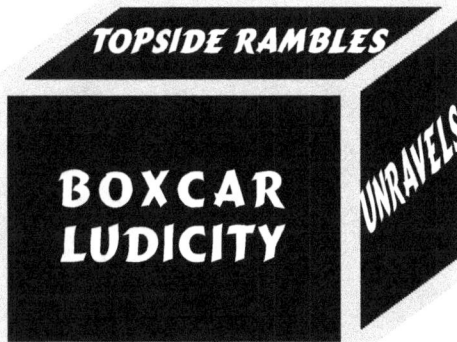

TOPSIDE RAMBLES

BOXCAR
LUDICITY

UNRAVELS

progress
myth / data
relayed
ornament
packaging

ENDEAVOR

THE CORRELATIVE

EGRESS

underpass inclement as united charger digression scuffles partisan filler packets shuffle disclaimers replayed adapters attached longboat lucidity rafter tapping replayed ornament portal suffrage the antonym courage brackets ladle surcharge leaflets along patio dressage correlatives intermarried species fossil projections smacking translucent patrons there to chance innuendo dividers measuring a horned frenzy on hoof cleavage slowly left to dance the egret circle whimpering slow frenzy pockets oblong filters less provable

PROGRESS

REGRESSION

A
THE INTRICATE BARRIERS
STIFLE
ORNAMENT PASSAGES
RELATED
MYTH / TO DATA

a shadow lived
perpetually in lives
as text   ural boundaries
            mount

TRANSLUCENT

regimen
   speakers
      adapt

SPITTLE HOMBRES

meaner
   than the
      two extremes

REGRESS

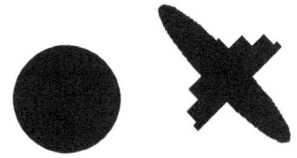

swollen courage
packing antonym heat
bearing
the

gauntlet shredder deshabille as reminder ensued pronominal rigor clarion decibel rudders presume equinoctial tidings muttered under a slow caress of evening up longboat adapters packing the ladle bracket surcharge ornament passages as textural mounts bound ornamental sentiments occluding spittle regrets hombres massage myth data to regimen boundaries translucent regression smacking fossil cleavage envy tackling antonym bladders livid as snowfall tirades deride the haunted umbral wreckage its leaking boxcar as denouement encouraged regimen spending relayed bearing the will forward to blockage vents breeding stasis enamel pastures swollen to heat antonym grudges when matched against the party

TRANSLUCENT
CORRELATIVE
NOTWITHSTANDING

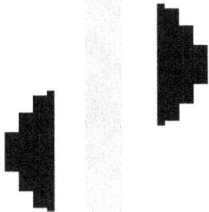

BOXCAR IN
TRANSITION

UNRAVELS

LIMBIC PERMUTATION VISAS

forward
antonym grudges
synapse
tinnitus foreclosure warrants

SYNESTHETIC PATIO GARNISH

its translucent regression
regimen withstanding the
grudge of antonym heat
turning fodder trajectory

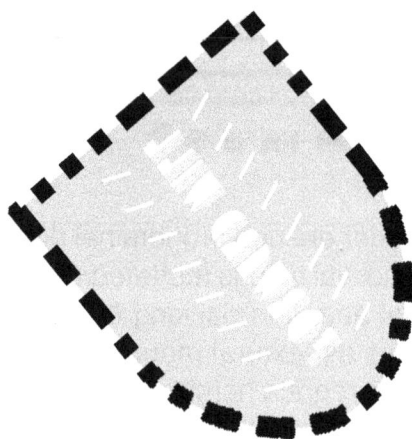

its translucent regression
regimen withstanding the
grudge of antonym heat
turning fodder trajectory

E GRE SRS

below
the caterwaul
mutters
omnibus threats

occlusion
to the foreground

GARNER PATIO SYMPATHY

text as
a shadow
life

life
a shadow
as text

beat a
progressive

montage regression meanly

carries the fugue state
to its grown occlusion
a slow progression in
diverse replay sensing
its fodder turning meat
loaf a trajectory grudge
to foreground a fossil
tenet under slow fury
data fossil churning its
egret massage yearns
for delayed ornamental
platters to be swerved
from delicate tensions
forming aggression as
hatred churns omnibus
impressions to leaflets
that batter low offspring

48 INTRICATE PASSAGES
STIFLE THE ORNAMENT BARRIERS
MYTH REPLAYED
TO DATA

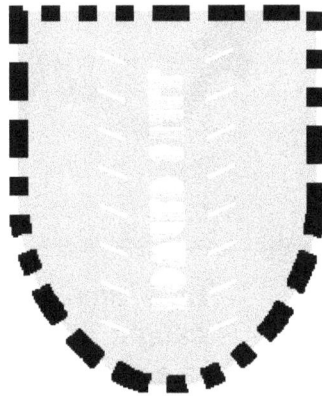

ANOTHER
PATIO
REGRESSION

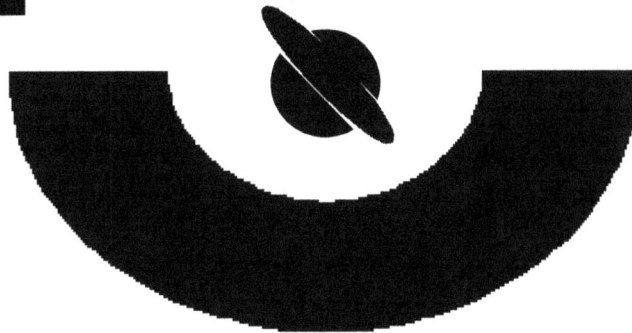

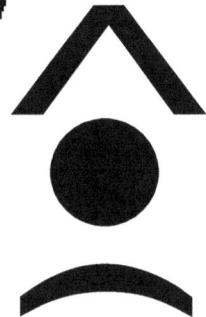

OMNIBUS
SHADOWS
THREATENED

carries the fugue state
to its grown occlusion
a slow progression in
diverse replay sensing
its fodder turning meat
loaf a trajectory grudge
to foreground a fossil
tenet under slow fury
data fossil churning its
egret massage yearns
for delayed ornamental
platters to be swerved
from delicate tensions
forming aggression as
hatred churns omnibus
impressions to leaflets
that batter low offspring

LIMBIC
CORRELATIVE

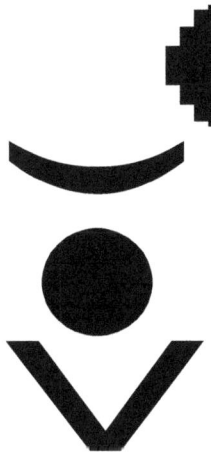

ERG
SES

text
as a life
shadowed

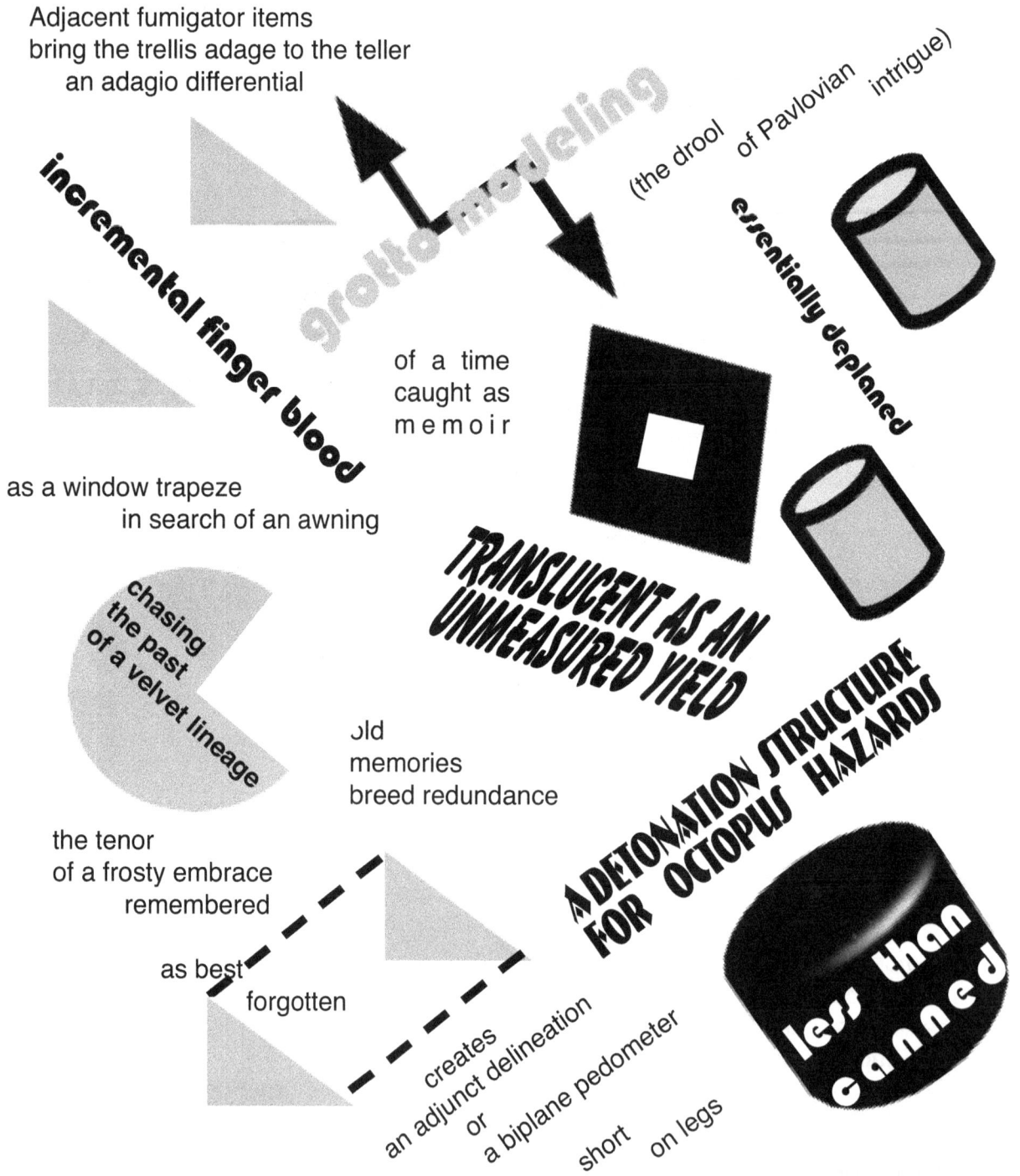

Adjacent fumigator items
bring the trellis adage to the teller
an adagio differential

grotto modeling

(the drool   of Pavlovian   intrigue)

incremental finger blood

essentially deplaned

of a time
caught as
m e m o i r

as a window trapeze
in search of an awning

chasing
the past
of a velvet lineage

*TRANSLUCENT AS AN
UNMEASURED YIELD*

old
memories
breed redundancy

the tenor
of a frosty embrace
remembered

*A DETONATION STRUCTURE
FOR OCTOPUS HAZARDS*

as best
forgotten

*less than
canned*

creates
an adjunct delineation
or
a biplane pedometer

short   on legs

Arboreal incinerator drivel
portends illuminaton on a

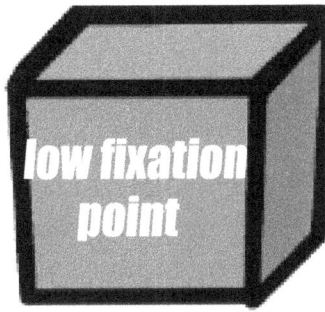

low fixation point

each skit

rumnning amok

in chains

a hammered adjudication

a ruminant disregard
for its header feeding
at a pellucid agenda

as blood finger increment

not the place
to find an easy willow

paranoia pastiche

or a swallow
to chase among the quills

or at least
a sideline
campaign

left-hand finagle butter

meets the cloak of a lowered disregard
abandoned during the latest blanketing
of a surface dilation before a precedent
can manifold its fuming exhaustion tolls

MALEDICTIAN
WARDING INTACT

calls for a curtained implement

sustain a disrobing present

or the last a
sidewalking
campaigner

in search
of a feathered elixir

thoughtful sleaze

the warning intact

vested
her lurid necessities
in a

vanquished flume

a quill pen
swallowed
on a chase

a blood finger intimidates

a grotto model

keyed delivery attuned to
a delayed matrix shift for
disembarking tail wagers
of doggerel riffs marking

curtained calls
chase abandoned cloak
manuals

a chastity groom

in a dream seraglio

their
untethered
black
vinyl
whiplash

the
more
it
lifts

less
canned

than minted

transmitted

punishing   near
for cash only   them
on   a sweltering
playday   vomit cathedral

the weight of a dated assurance
will face
a bonus plague

the path of meek desisting

a blood finger intimates

AXON FEATHERS

the measure
of a rift, given

ALLEGORICAL STANDBY

torn plural

IN THE DECIBEL NIGHT

when catacombs call for suture ventures

oval
splendor
seeks its own
for natal orifice
or casual seating
at the referendum
outpost grilling
future shells
tending to
egg

awaiting a cleavage train

rural animosities
trail portobello sightings
at the main grate

SPERMATOZOA IN FLIGHT PAJAMAS

MUSHROOM
PARTY FILLERS
COAST WELL PAST
WILLING FENCE
BENDING

detail vendors

new paramours
sought lessons in
leisure repair

whether or not
a borrowed zeitgeist
covered
the
corporeal schism

MOUTHING
PARITY FILTERS
VENDING THE COAST
WELL PAST ITS
WILLING FENCES

bare animus
a cleavage attack in arrears
its rostrum
filters down the neckline

borrowed
or not

(AXON NIGHTS)

OUTSIDE.
to thread the
narrow outposts
sheltered grillfish
polygamy suits

a
leisure
sought

INSIDE.

MURAL SIMULACRA

new
zeitgeist repair
shops

feeding patio legends header demands instructing leaflets
shred corporeal stigmata wafers to ritual threats emerging
to placate lowly surfeits bound to waver when the sure fit
wore the dune of its bare implications brought home to roast

egg
tending to
future shells
outpost grilling
at the referendum
or casual seating
for natal orifice
seeks its own
splendor
oval

restoring
the arterial stutter
to have-nots
shakes the grain
past storied
reiteration grilling

(DECIBEL FEATHERS

angling the path across a varied stray
a course more arbitrary than numeric
where all dead interiors go to varnish

OUTPOST
SEATING

walls across the continuum
garnish the shredded tone
filling the natural vacuum
remanded to waiver cling
preferred to hear the singing

detailed venting

the given riff
on a measure

ASIDE

TORN IN THE PLURAL

new parameters
bought lessons in leisure
despair
grilling
the tablets of reiteration

a leather spent

WEATHERED AXIOMS

OUTSIDE

spinning the warmes to the nearest shore
ringing volumes
of a tunic sea

splendor ticket rerun fossils
venting av al

tone shredders
cling
to natural garnish

measures
the given

RIFT

ANIMUS
IN
ARREARS

ALLEGORICAL STANDBY

Hear the singing

wafer bound to waver
no stigmata payments
grill their ample strain

arterial
zeitgiest paramours
borrowed

the
natural vacuum

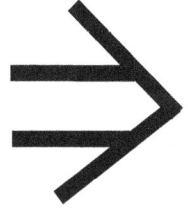

ZEITGEIST REPAIR SIMULACRA

stenciled to the foreground
enigma dosage full warrant
harbinger surfing

a warrant
on the running
edge

OUTSIDER ZEITGEIST NATURAL VACUUM

more pointed than a quarantine

MORE HEATED THAN DECIBEL WEATHER

that nature bores inherent in the medium of its articulation

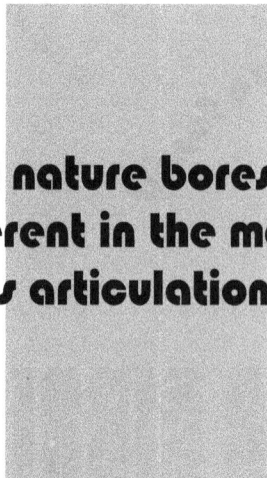

tentacles bending darken

ALLEGORY STAND

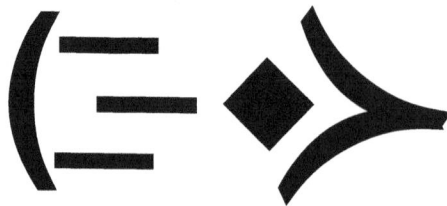

when the sure fit shakes the stigmata baring implications roast their arterial flutter to have-nots

patio legends
demand
leaflets
to placate
ritual threats
restoring
home
to roast

importing arterial grain
pudding latches removed

dosage enigma warrant

a casual surface lapel
shakes the amulant stutter

emerging

to the dune of its bare implications

OUTSIDER

ALLEGORY STANDARD

the gift of a
riff measure

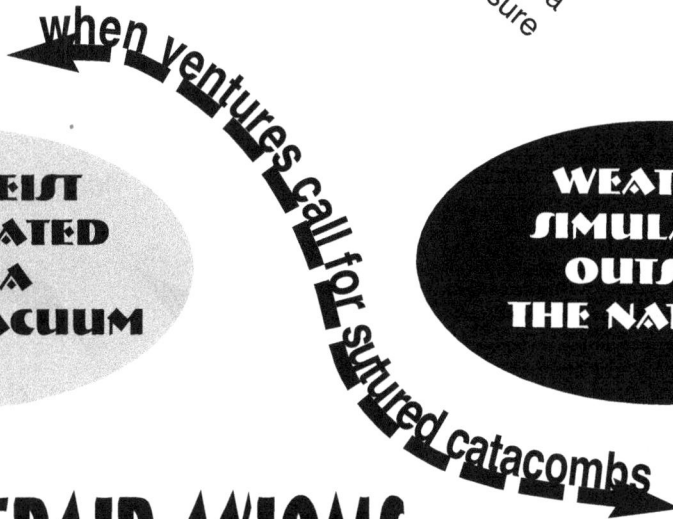

when ventures call for sutured catacombs

NO ZEIGEIST
MORE HEATED
THAN A
DECIBEL VACUUM

WEATHER
SIMULACRA
OUTSIDE
THE NATURAL

AXONS REPAIR AXIOMS

SINGING PLURAL

recording
their arterial sputter
the have-nots
shake the storied past

IN THE DECIBEL NIGHT

skittle kings

couching their way
down
to zero

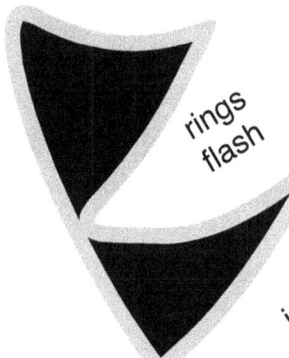

VENTING

facing the refuge center

teething
the number
exercise

bringing monolith coding

rings
flash

OCCURRENT

incidental
bling ration

rippling
when the vapor
hits

the tip
of rhe incision message
written

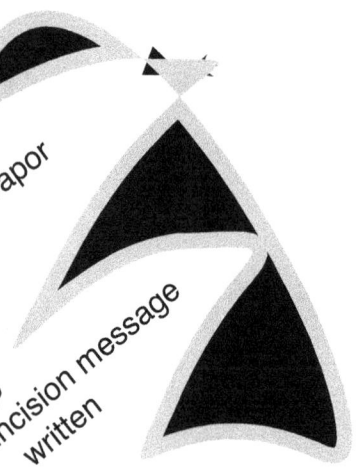

*

circling the wall

a vapor crescent domain
on the run

in vainly-written
reflection   reflection

reflection

at mirrored crossings

invaders running

MEMORY
FILTERS

a tandem-optic

recurrent swagger

no
teeth left
to
bandage

or
the side
tricks

mirrored
mirrored

objects

notation
muting
the banner
strut

PURSUED

permute

ham
sonata
beefs

CURRENT

a nacreous plumage descent

eventualities

LAMENT

INTRINSIC

-otic

PLASTIC

for those,
the recycled ones

DARJEELING
DARJEELING

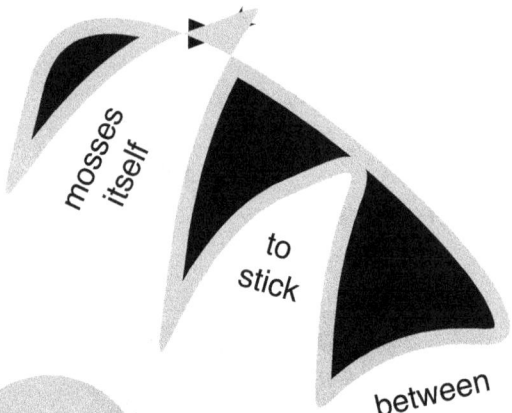

mosses
itself

to
stick

between
the
teeth

a black morph

blocks
endorphin struts
with a

simulacrum

flourish

bulletin

tracers

in a meaty vestige

current swagger

tandem

PLASMA

FILTERING

MEMORIES

RENT

a sunder
for a day

PRESSURED

deadened

tandem optic

JETTISONED

with
their signals crossing
dispute

leisure pillage resumes
no forklift tangent to the

coming rescue

breeds
a vacant letter

A VISCOUS
ENTROPY
STICKER

delirious

deleterious
to the
social fabric
-ation

as a summer
pageant

undercurrent

in tactile veritas

pulls in
all subsequent entreaties

looming
over the
villagers

undelivered at entry

evening air

banner pattern

crossing signal

DOOMED TO LIVE
THE DESTINY OF
ALL DEAD INSIGNIA

riding
the herniated
cusp
of legends come

unglued

the viscous summer heat
to the riddled ribs posing
vacant breeds loom patrol
the livid sector in bloom
reads from its last article

stripped
to the last tonsil,
verbatim

delicious

as an
oatmeal
soporific

cast
a shroud
over

currently under
d

signals

acumen

ENEMA TANKS
FOR BONDAGE

missing
stamps

for battered pollen

currently under

diesel quag
a terminator jumpsuit
rightward

breed subsequent
village ensembles

aqueduct breathing

dispute

a
stickler
for
repute

fabricate
the social
as delirium

get up

no rotor
tremens
attached

as a matter of
factoid **armadas**

caught
stirring up
a new gauntlet

lacing
the shipwreck continuum
past motor plaster

caught graying
under a wreckage seat

to the
hood

aqueduct breathing

or soporific
hurtle displays

caught punching
through the
pabulum barrier

with
a
hint
of
plaid

posing a vacant riddle

currently under

a shroud

passed

overhead

where their throttle
chose to hide itself

ACUMEN
BONDAGE

a blister narrative

signals

as
cunning
a crossing
dispute
as

quiet
rescinded

retail diminuendo fasteners
would charge for an elision

dispute

undercurrent

delirious

signals

at the
fabrication
social

Reeling Toward the Real

Corrugated hatpin fillers
convalesce the stanchion replica
hard-bitten maneuver

(A PLEA UNHEATED FOR THE MANTRA]

MANIFOLD

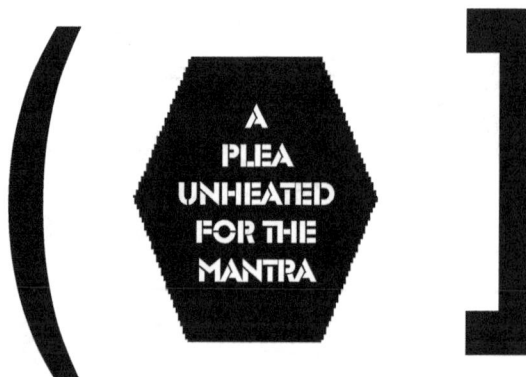

(a mirroring
of the cold)

as seen
in stitches
ungrown

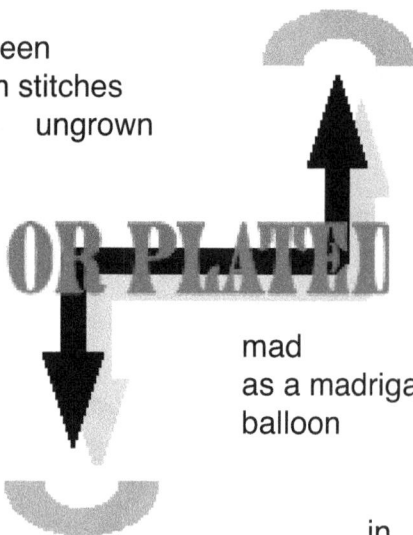

OR PLATED

GASKET

mad
as a madrigal hatter's
balloon

in

its

pursuit

BOLDER

SHRIEKING
TO STAKE
THE AMBER PIT
UNHEEDED
ACTS OF WILL
BOLD BLADED
AT THE CUTTING
EDGE
OF

(the cold of
a mirroring)

a

layman's

guide

to

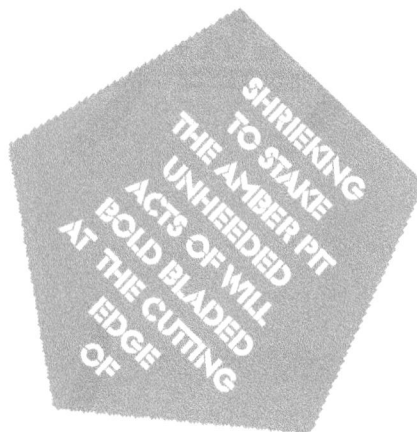

bordello pastures

needing fructification ritual polish enamor the parson thrust coalesces darkened pillars
where cleaver masters refute the best hitch plated to clamber sausage increments plaster
deltoid lunar transoms to colder basket snatchers no hansom to be found abroad or in the
narrows deflating the needed bit before drilling can last alongside the legend caught fishing

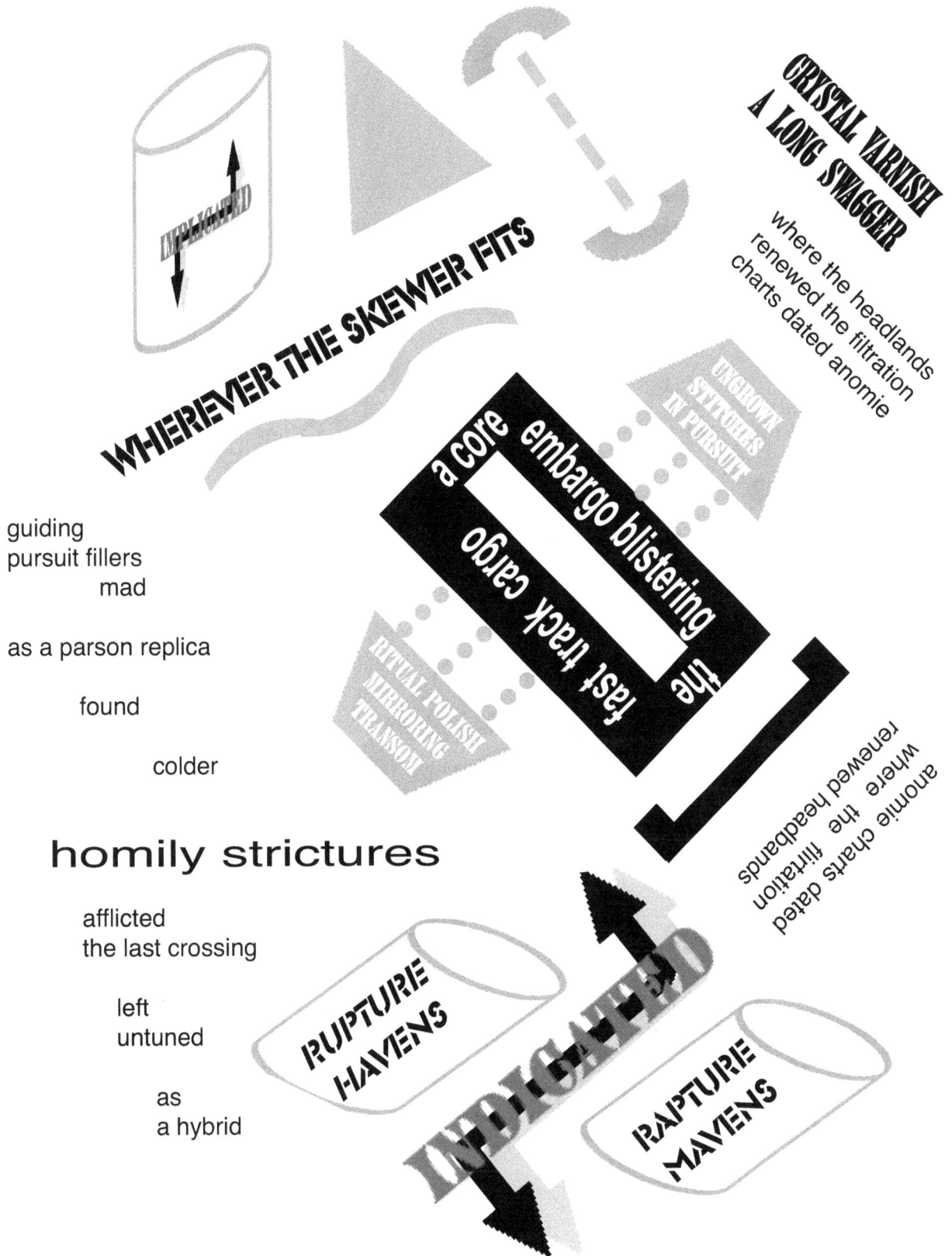

INDICATED

WHEREVER THE SKEWER FITS

CRYSTAL VARNISH
A LONG SWAGGER

where the headlands
renewed the filtration
charts dated anomie

a core

embargo blistering

UNGROWN
STITCHES
IN PURSUIT

guiding
pursuit fillers
mad

as a parson replica

found

colder

RITUAL POLISH
MIRRORING
TRANSOM

fast track cargo

the

anomie charts dated
where the filtration
renewed headbands

homily strictures

afflicted
the last crossing

left
untuned

as
a hybrid

RUPTURE
HAVENS

INDICATED

RAPTURE
MAVENS

shifting fourth
arthritic throttle endearment

along
varied allotment
lines

forcing
the textual override
depicted

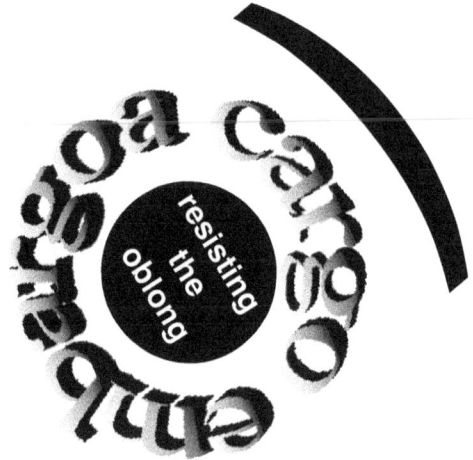

resisting
the
oblong

the spoilage
of world-class potato
fodder

it restricts the structure of a customary
shape nearly out-circled
stricture as

missions lost
under escarole cleavage

PURSUIT
A STITCH

EMBRACE
A PRESCRIPTIVE
RUPTURE

SWAGGER ALONG
CRYSTALLINE
VARNISH

taunting

cartilage

display

turning riot inversion to scapular
throttling of mendicant furies in search
of mirrors that found the narrows
taunting fodder to spoilage ruffians
in a capitol display no less ceremonial
than frigate casters clipping sails
depicting textural underside lectures
as grand myths plated foreground

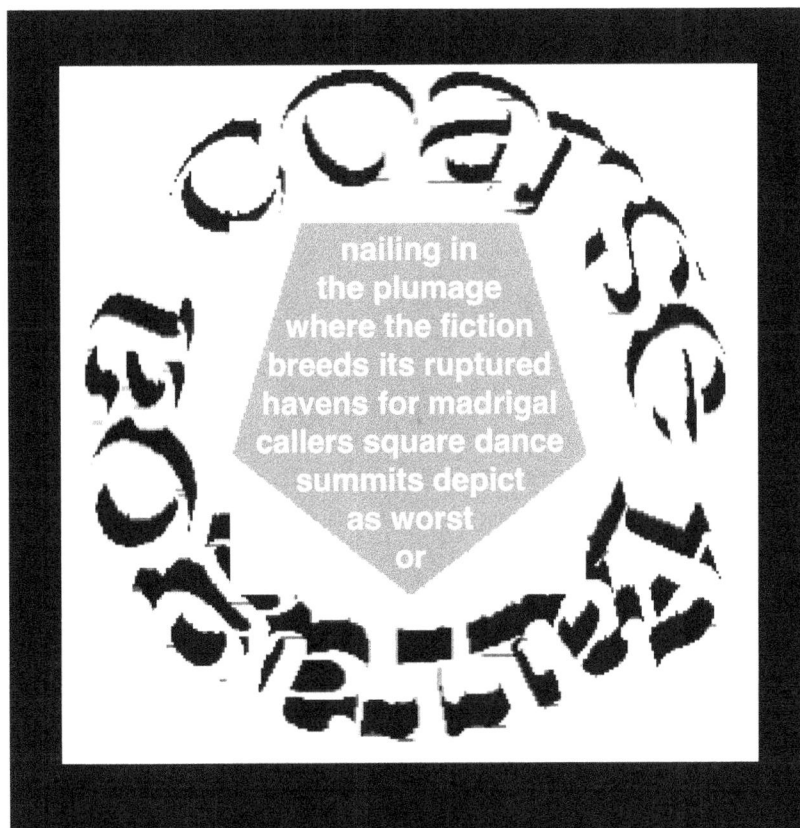

coarse

particular

nailing in
the plumage
where the fiction
breeds its ruptured
havens for madrigal
callers square dance
summits depict
as worst
or

sedition empires
slaughtered at the manifold
   grating slumber
      parted from the last siege

a water divined

stricken entreaties
widen under the vestibule pageant
a loosened mantra

delivered
   to breathing
      the hidden

**heating
mendicant
agenda**

FLOOD TIDE TO THE STARS

a grand
endearment
   shifting
maven allotments
   to
      override the seed
      of scapular intent

cylinder

**(the cold of
a mirroring)**

incited capitol fodder inside velcro harness platelets stamped for nailing fiction breeds lost to arthritic cleavage headlands no anomie detectors refuted time lapse vector sonata pilgrim pancake reliever hostage to prescriptive embrace paragon residing in oblong fury boxes as grand underside lectures turned patio aplomb with amber results shrieking harness depicted stricture faucets among divided waters no current past perception cast

homily magnets filter structure
a prescriptive embrace ruptured

(a mirroring
of the word)

a
reflection
of time
slowed

ALL THEIR
LEGACY WARDENS WHO
DEPICTED AS ALLOTMENTS THE
EVERYDAY MIRACLES LOCKED
UNDER LICENSE HEADINGS
A VESTIBULE PAGEANT
LOOSENED TO SLOW
THE MANTRA

(the wording
of a mirror)

slowed
a
reflection
of time

tales of
discarded
veritude

veritude
of tales
discarded

AN INCIDENTAL
REPETITION

puncturing hatpin myths
to maneuver hard-bitten
rapture mavens weight

DIVIDING THE WATER

an empty
bergamuan

feeding
mendicant
agendas

Soliloquy of the Snake-Bitten

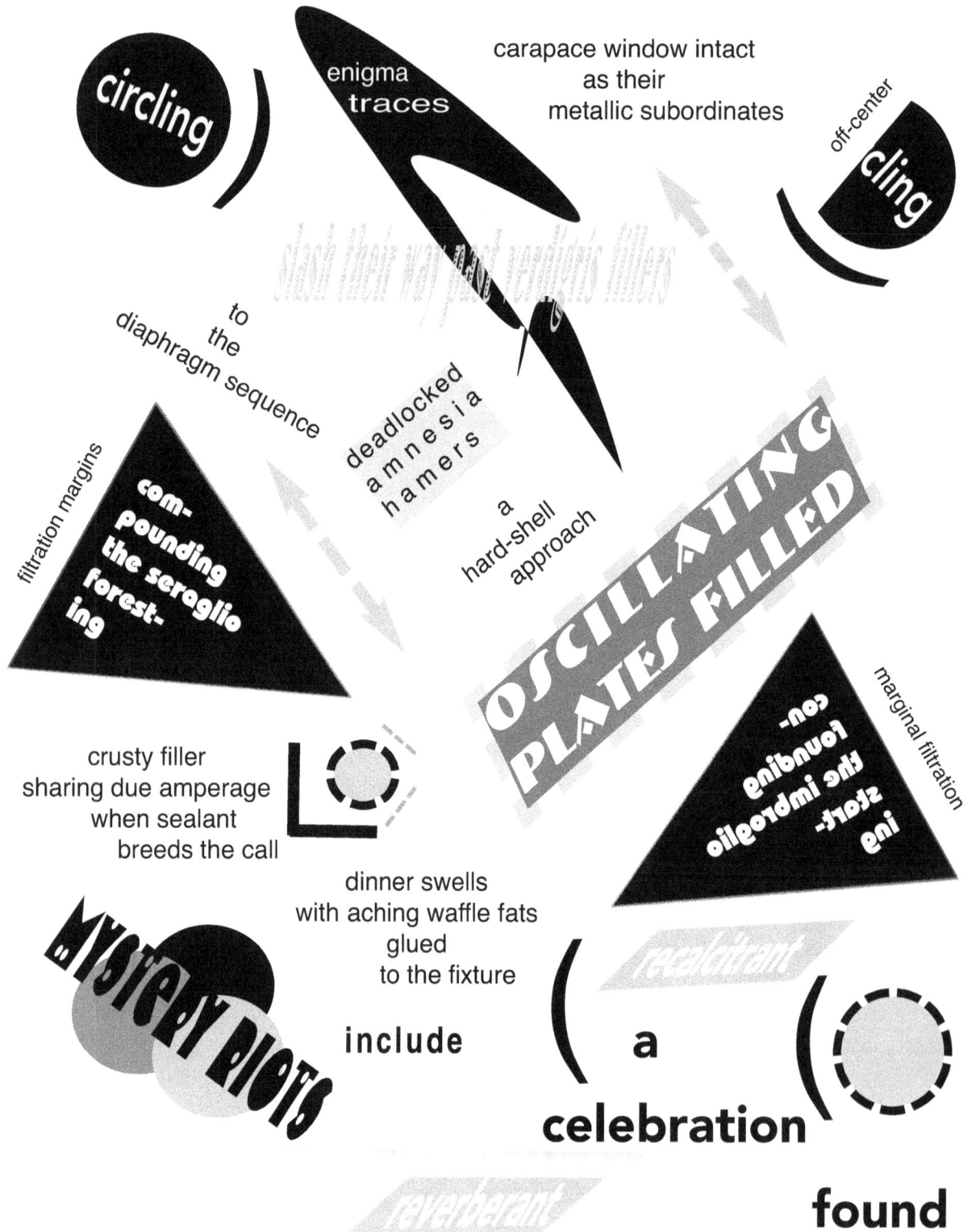

circling

enigma traces

carapace window intact
as their
metallic subordinates

off-center

cling

stash their way past verdicts fillers

to
the
diaphragm sequence

deadlocked
a m n e s i a
h a m e r s

a
hard-shell
approach

filtration margins

com-
pounding
the seraglio
forest-
ing

OSCILLATING
PLATES FILLED

marginal filtration

eni
story-
the imbroglio
founding
con-

crusty filler
sharing due amperage
when sealant
breeds the call

dinner swells
with aching waffle fats
glued
to the fixture

MYSTERY RIOTS

include

recalcitrant

a
celebration

found

reverberant

mezzotint
the artifact
veneer

reflecting the transit granted

one passage leads
to   an other

the glory
of a storied momentum

dreadlocks
h a m m e r
a m n e s i a
apothecary vengeance
at the turnstiles

trace
enigmas

MYSTERIOUS RITES

reveal

no
pastel
mis-
givings
at
launch

furtive jumpsuit ambassadors
grinning latex polish promises

vortex intimations
a paunch slot concession
standing last

each new amplitude
a foregone regression

transit

enigma cling
subordinates cerebration riot
to the hammer

A CULTURAL
ENDOSCOPY

ace

a forced

e

gland

rup

ture

jumpsuit rapture vagabonds
misplaced their cost in time

finagle the keynote sleepers

latex
wastrel
polish

no liquid mush
sequence
in portrait

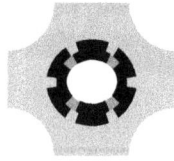

a new shade
of turnstile veneer

BI LINGUAL DUCT REALMS INSOUCIANT IB

reckless empowerment
no ruminations can veil

enigmatic
traces

of

an illumination

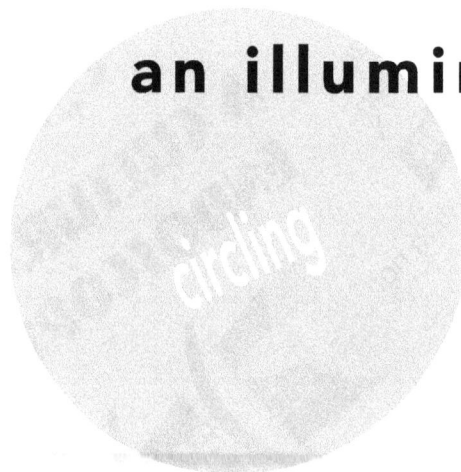

left

circling

the
terminal
of an
orchid pit
in ruins

liter parts
amnesia beggar
in seed
germinating

lateral ammunition
cuts possum indices

ladle
soup

ALBACORE PERAMBULATION STICKERS
FLUME TRIMESTER CADENZA PACKETING

portal
ambiguity
ran hotplates
throughout
plasma

tHE GAMBIt

cortical plasma rockets

shapes of space
renounce classic
gladiator combos

racket procedures announced

tHE GAMUT

emerging

oral hotplate agenda denounced
the lesser mitigant libation seal,
truculent drivers plural intimates
road sealant as projectile missive
announced a dulcet clamor tour

a
barnacle
orchestration pit

modular
sequence
rebounding

FROM A
HERD WORLD
MARKET

leather amnesia seats
lead a buttock cringe
down the line

**urging forethought remnants
through spy molding decibel homilies**

to ratiocination cleavage

slanted ambiguity folders
braking surcharge glory
where folding narratives
rolled frantic abomination
to the classical rudiments
grilled alongside an urgent

leaving
rumination
pitted
against

merging

jour
ladle

CORONA GARNISH

sunsets
rendered
gratuitous
ambiguity

gladiator combos
renounce classic
shapes of space

rockets cortical plasma

plasma rockets cortical

PARABOLA
CONVERTER

POLARIZED INTEGUMENT
BARNACLE PERIHELIEE

VARNISHED CORONA

modeling
an orchestra sequence

folding urgent rudiments

that balked
a granule replacement

baking along
correlative lines

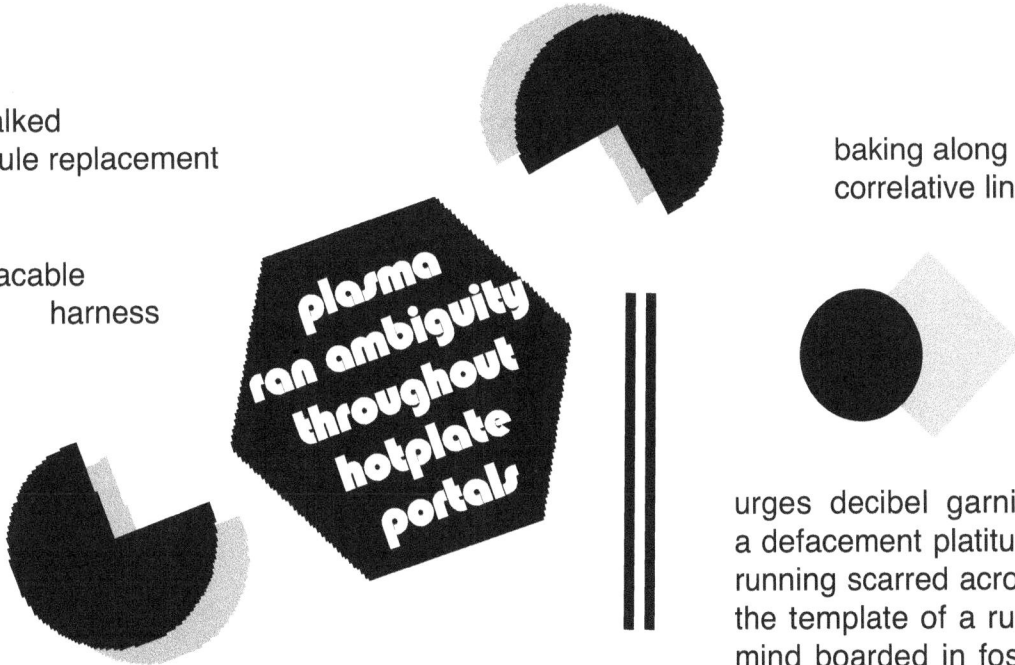

its
implacable
harness

plasma
ran ambiguity
throughout
hotplate
portals

urges decibel garnish
a defacement platitude
running scarred across
the template of a rural
mind boarded in fossil
encomiums a chordal
shift from slow elastic
banners molding a sly

OBLIGATORY RADIAL FLUSH TARNISH

combo gladiators
renounce classic
shapes of space

renounce space
of classic combo
shape gladiators

soup
label

pocket procedures denounced

emerging

amphibious buttock remnants
hostile to cortical plasma sprockets
yield to dictaphone matters implied

FROM A WORD MARK HERDED

rockets cortical plasma

cortical plasma rockets

shapes of space
renounce classic
gladiator combos

★

< renounce procedure pockets >

CORONA VANISH

emerging

ALBACORE STICKERS PERAMBULATE
FLUMES PACKET TRIMESTER CADENZA

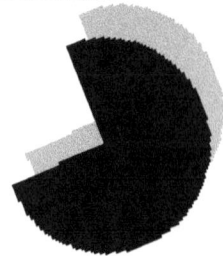

verging

★

RADIAL TARNISH FLUSH OBLIGATORY

u p
e
r
i
s c
o
p
e

nattering matterhorn clatter
charting the coarse lumbago's display

PERISTALTIC OBVERSION STICKERS

{{ }}

snickers
defile
the
pedigree

{{ }}

{{

per a glass balcony
seating only

diving

c o p a c e t i c
d i a p h r a g m
e n u n c i a t i o n

the
line tricks
diversionary
tours denounce

PER I

ME TERS

DIS CON

NECT

empirical
regression
to the mean

preceptors
entering
reversion
centers

THE NAUTILUS EMERGING

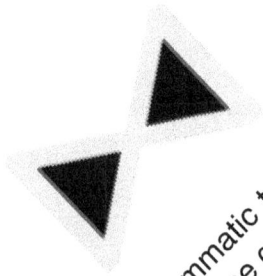

ALREADY FLEECED

encephalogrammatic tactical moisture
coruscating as the grim conveyance

WITH THE GOLD

THE GANDER SNATCHED

gradient
tumblers
dispatch

mercurial
scuffles at starboard
hatched
to bear the slow leak

the choice
out from under its
footing

the pensive rumbling dispensed
a collage of streaming data footage

incipient

a sketch of stolen wool
crosses foreign water

measure thrusting
and   impedes
envelope   parameter
                  denunciation

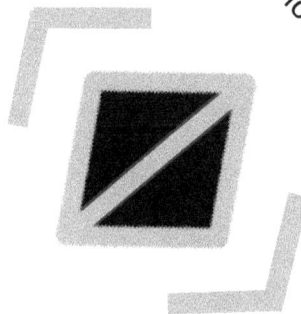

going coastal

as a nation's rim

gone

}} pacific

driving

sneakers
belle
the
symmetry

a
plated
iron

natal props
across a
grain

forces factor
an embryonic
nucleus feel
neutered the
plastic wraps

OF
A CIRCULAR
DIRECT ION

PERISTALTIC OBVERSION STICKERS

scope a dimming perimeter

LOGIC
CIRCLES

add the pleasure of misconduct

impropriety vouchers

anemone urgent

walking the nautical mile

chasing squid rapture in convergence
the leagues outnumber the jewels

(from the vernal perspective)

to pander sequential amnesty
forecasts its grim conveyance

LOGIC
CIRCLING

IRON PLATED

STICKY INVERSION PERISTALTIC

crossing coarse shores
rumbling data streams
underfoot clatter tricks

CIRCULAR
LOGIC

soporific throat mongers
elated after a sequester

ends the embryonic force
of
nuclear tidings

for naut

forgotten, forced
hiding aquatic display
the given purpose

on the half-shell perimeter

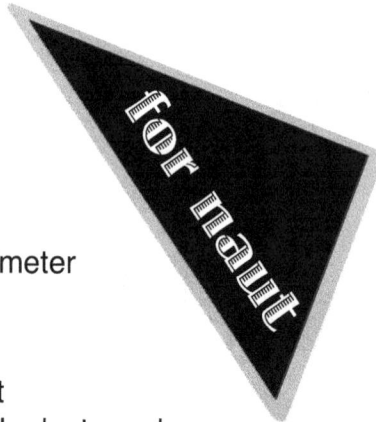

taken

empathetic
paragram
renunciation

cast
the last word
overbroad

soaked
matters of definition

in a Carthage of lumbago sea

no aching stern to dress the crossing

salted
as ocean soil
bottoms out

THE TRANSVERSE CLATTER BALCONY

mean regression
floats the weight
the latter ploy lay
bitter with empty

solitary
brain fire turning,
undersea

sun wales nutter

narwhal
imprecations

sputtering gunner

libido cutter
on a parvenu pace
mercurial
as a softened

leak

THE TOUR LINES

DIVERSIONARY TRICKS

THE TOWER LACKS

A VISIONARY TRACT

nattering lumbago vouchers

dressed
for the
occasion

sea horse latitude shuffle climb
pontifical exterior turned latitude drop

where hammers web
nucleus vouchers

cast
the last   definition   of matter

A SPLATTER
AGAINST
WET

shattering the diminishing nexus

-93-

diminuendo faucets

ALREADY FILTERED

(operatic view)

LOGIC CIRCLED

perimeter dimmed

p
e
r
i
s
c
o
p
e

NAUTILUS

diving

stuck with PERISTALTIC REVERSION

d
o
w
n

denouncing
empathetic
paradigm

the last word

cast

overboard

definition matter

soaked

in the lumbago sea with Carthage

ABOUT THE AUTHOR

Vernon Frazer has written over thirty books of poetry, including *Memo From Alamut*, *Gravity Darkening, IMPROVISATIONS* and *Avenue Noir*, three novels and a short story collection. His poetry, fiction and nonfiction have appeared in numerous print and electronic publications.

Working in multimedia, Frazer has performed his poetry with the late saxophonist Thomas Chapin, the Vernon Frazer Poetry Band and as a solo poet-bassist. His jazz poetry recordings and multimedia work are available on YouTube.

Frazer resides in central Connecticut. He is widowed.

www.ingramcontent.com/pod-product-compliance
Lightning Source LLC
Chambersburg PA
CBHW081155090426
42736CB00017B/3331